Reform Your Animal Shelter

NOW!

The citizens' guide to animal shelter reform.

by

Jacki Moss
Diane Finl

Copyright 2017 Jacki Moss – All Rights Reserved
Lewisburg, TN

Library of Congress Control Number: 2017914451

Reform Your Animal Shelter Now!

by Jacki Moss and Diane Finley

TABLE OF CONTENTS

Preface

Biographies
Jacki Moss
Diane Finley

Dedication

Special thank you to:

Teri Cox – President, Animal Rescue Assistance Team Tennessee (ARATT), and all the intrepid ARATT team members (past and present) for their continual commitment to saving homeless and unwanted animals in Tennessee.

All Aboard Animal Rescue (AAAR) in Middle Tennessee for their compassionate dedication to rescuing animals and for sharing their Adoption Contract with us.

Nathan Winograd for his continuing leadership in the No-Kill movement.

Preface

We could cite the kill shelter stats ad nauseum, but you already know them. You've seen them first hand. We have all shed torrents of tears and spewed righteous anger at those in charge of local hellhole pounds – sometimes euphemistically called "shelters" – until exhaustion. And still they murder innocent animals day after day.

Now what?

Now is the time for action.

No more hand-wringing. No more accepting the status quo. No more allowing our tax dollars to be used to needlessly snuff out the lives of the animals in the care and control of your local animal control pound.

Reform Your Animal Shelter Now! is a citizens' guide to help you galvanize or force reform where it has to happen: locally. Local citizens must take charge and either educate and inform the people who are in charge of your local pound into reforming, or you must make it easier for them to reform than to withstand your incessant, persistent, unrelenting onslaught of reform demands.

It won't be quick. It won't be easy. It won't be painless, but most things worth working for aren't quick, easy, or painless. When you're ready to give up, ask yourself if the next day would have been the one that turned the corner. When you're ready to give up, think about the lives lost every single day going forward because you gave up. When you're ready to give up, read another chapter in the book and keep going.

The key is: do not give up. Stop ONLY when you have succeeded.

Let's get to work.

Dedication

This book is dedicated to the thousands of rescuers who are giving everything they have, every day, in every way, to save homeless, abused, neglected, and unwanted animals.

We've been there. We ARE there. We feel your pain. We've cried your tears and screamed your curses. We've had to balance our families with our rescue passion. We've been ridiculed, insulted, threatened, and called crazy. We've won many battles, but still hurt from those we didn't win.

We've saved a lot of animals and lost many, too. We remember them all. They are all indelibly etched into our hearts. Their spirits give us strength to go forward when we think we can't even breathe, let alone see another animal with a broken spirit and broken body.

We know you. We ARE you.

We cherish you. We respect you. We want to give you not only hope for a better world, but some tools to help you bring it into reality.

Most of all, we thank you.

Now go out there and kick some ass! MAKE the change happen!

Jacki and Diane

Jacki Moss Biography

Jacki Moss rescued her first stray when she was five years old. She heard a puppy whimpering, found it, and decided to save it. She knew her mom wouldn't allow her to officially have it, so she hid it in a large (safe) drainage pipe nearby and took care of it several days until her mom followed her one day and found out her secret.

That was her gateway rescue. Since then, she has personally rescued dozens of dogs and cats, and been involved in rescues by other individuals and entities.

But in 2010, her rescue efforts became intensely focused when she became aware of a tiny, pitiful puppy in her local pound. She saw it on Facebook and decided to go get it. She had never been to the local pound before and was horrified and sickened at what she saw there. The animals were in makeshift wire cages, had bloody paws, were crammed in together and fighting, had no heat, and were covered in their own feces and urine. The pound typically kept the animals the mandatory three days and then promptly killed them.

She vowed to make a difference for those babies. She partnered with another rescuer, Teri Cox, who was already trying to make a difference. Together, they and a team of equally dedicated citizens, including Diane Finley, FORCED reform at the hellhole pound. Everyone told them it couldn't be done. That it had been tried a dozen times and failed. That the dogs would be killed in retaliation. That the government would "go after" them. That they would be wasting their time.

They were right about the obstacles. They were not right that it could not be done. They did it.

They did it in a small, rural, good-ol'-boy town that had a woefully under-funded pound and a government determined to not change a damn thing about it.

It was difficult and heartbreaking, but they prevailed. Today, that former place of cruelty and murder is a model shelter in the true sense of the word. It is very nearly no-kill, safe and comfortable for the animals, and an asset to the community.

The citizens group had to use every tool they could imagine to force change, but they did it. Those efforts and techniques are the genesis of this book.

They did it. You can, too.

Diane Finley Biography

Diane Finley has spent her entire life with animals, growing up with a menagerie of rescues – no stray was ever turned away from her family's home. Animal welfare and rescue has always been her passion, and she has devoted many years to helping the unwanted dogs and cats in Tennessee and throughout the South.

She has also worked with wildlife rescue, but dogs and cats have been her main focus. Diane was heavily involved in the transformation of a middle Tennessee high-kill shelter to a now no-kill shelter, and now works with shelters and rescues on a daily basis with saving animals and finding approved new homes. She also operates a cat rescue and sanctuary at her home, which she currently shares with two dogs and sixteen cats.

Chapter 1
THE Most Important Thing

THE most important thing you can do to force shelter reform is never give up. Never. Not just give it a good try and give up. NEVER give up. Never.

Yes, many have tried before you. Yes, there are some people who you have made angry or they have made you angry. Yes, there are people who you believe will never let change happen. Yes, some of the people in charge are heartless. Yes, there's no budget. Yes, they will retaliate. Yes, they will threaten. Yes, very few, if any, people will join you in this fight. Yes, it's just you against the world.

Now, forget all that and move on. If it was going to be easy, it would have already been done. Now it's up to you.

If you have tried the professional, work-through-the-channels approach and been stonewalled, then that is your signal to start putting on the pressure until change happens. Get that? Until change happens. Not until you get tired. Not until you get frustrated. Not until you've cried a river of tears.

Keep pushing until change happens.

Be prepared for a long, painful, time-consuming, labor-intensive slog. And when you get discouraged remember two things:

1. The faces of the animals whose lives depend on you to not give up and,
2. Giving up is exactly what the government wants you to do and *counts* on you to do.

If they were going to have a humane, no-kill pound, they would have already done it. So that means that people long before you have tried and failed at forcing reform. The government officials know that and count on that happening again. They rope-a-dope; they procrastinate; they say it takes time; they slow-walk everything; they say there is no budget; they say their hands are tied; they wait you out; they threaten you; they threaten to kill animals; they may kill animals; then they won and animals kept being murdered.

But you CAN force change if you don't give up. It may take weeks or months or even years, but eventually, when they believe that you will ALWAYS be there to expose them and to be a thorn in their side, eventually they will decide that reforming their hellhole pound is good business for them. Don't expect them to reform out of the goodness of their hearts. If that was going to happen, it would have already happened.

You have to make it in their best interest to reform. It is in their best interest to:

- Avoid bad publicity locally.
- Avoid bad publicity statewide.
- Avoid bad publicity nationally.
- Keep citizens from snooping in their financial records.
- Avoid time spent on responding to Freedom of Information Act (FOIA) requests.
- Keep state officials from snooping in their records.
- Avoid dealing with the same problems again and again in council meetings.
- Avoid being embarrassed by weekly protests.
- Avoid being embarrassed by a petition that goes viral and shames them worldwide.
- Avoid lawsuits from citizens.
- Work with citizens to become no-kill, because it makes them look like heroes.
- Work with citizens to become no-kill, because it is the fiscally responsible thing to do.

Here's a word of warning. Once you start a full-court press to force reform, you MUST NOT give up. If you give up, it will further embolden the people in charge to dig in their heels for the next time. They see that you gave it your best shot, and they weathered the storm and won. They will become even more of a bully. Every time a group starts a push for reform and quits, it strengthens the bullies.

In fact, if you start and then give up, the people in charge may then see it as a license to REGRESS and further deny citizens' rights and to run the pound without regard for what their citizens may think. That usually means even more cruel and inhumane practices and even less adherence to laws.

So either be in it until you get what you want for the future pound victims, or step away until you are ready to fight until you win.

Chapter 2
Your Right to Complain

So they have closed your shelter's access to the public. Or they have a gag order on volunteers and threaten to fire them if they don't comply. What do you do?

Section 1983 gives you the **right** to complain about your government-run departments **and** to demand that abuses be addressed *and corrected.* Furthermore, you also have the right to document and disseminate your complaints of wrongdoing.

An animal control facility (pound or shelter) is a government-funded agency. That means that it is funded by *your* tax dollars. That means that you have RIGHTS, even though you will probably be told otherwise.

The officials in charge of the shelter will throw all kinds of excuses, reasons, threats, and other bull to keep you out and under control, but the bottom line is that they have NO RIGHT to exclude you from access to this public facility **because you complain about them**. There is nothing special about an animal control facility staff or government leadership that allows them to be above the law nor to deny you your First Amendment right of free speech.

Under the First Amendment, speaking out about a government-run animal shelter is considered political speech, and therefore protected.

Of course, no government official with common sense will admit that they are banning you or infringing on your Free Speech because of your complaints. So they lie. Every time they lie, though, they run the risk of creating a cause against them. Your task is to document their violation of your free speech rights.

Whenever possible, make sure to document their refusals to allow you exercise your free speech. Even if you cannot record or video a conversation or sign, immediately document the date, the time, the location, the people involved, and what they said.

Common excuses (aka lies)

- Safety – They claim that they don't allow citizens into the pound for the safety of the public. Then the questions are: what, specifically, about the pound is so unsafe, and why is the government spending your tax dollars running a facility that has unsafe conditions and is so poorly managed?
- They are understaffed – They probably *are* understaffed. That's why they should create a volunteer program so volunteers can help take care of the animals and find homes and rescues for them. They make your case for a volunteer program if they tell you this.
- They just plain don't have to – Now that's where they are wrong. You need to enlighten them about their duties under the law. While you're at it, make sure that the mayor, council people, and city and county attorneys are enlightened, as well.

Threats

- You will be banned from being a volunteer – You have a right to help. Period.
- They will kill all the animals in the pound and/or change their policy and go to all-kill if you continue to press the issue - They might do this. But they are probably doing a lot of this unnecessary murder anyway. You might lose more babies. But in the long run, if you don't change how the pound is operating, this will continue forever. More animals will be killed

until you force change. If they do this, then make sure that the media jumps on it ASAP.

- They will sue you for defamation – The absolute defense for defamation is if what you are saying or writing is the truth. Let them know that you have the proof and to bring it on and that you will contact an attorney and let the media know.

You have a Constitutional right to have access to that government facility, and you don't have to have an attorney to exercise that right. Of course, if you have an attorney to assist you or your group in educating the people in charge, all the better. If you need an attorney, call your nearest American Civil Liberties Union and ask for a referral.

Gag order on volunteers

Many shelters will allow volunteers to help them on the condition that they sign a Volunteer Agreement or a similar document that outlines the rules by which they must abide. While a government agency does have a right to require an agreement that demands confidentiality of information, that information is supposed to protect other citizens. The names, addresses and other personal information gathered at the shelter should be kept confidential. That makes sense.

Where shelters run afoul of the Volunteer Agreement is if they also include a gag order on volunteers sharing information about the shelter. They often threaten that if a volunteer speaks with anyone, especially media, about the conditions of the shelter or the animals, they will immediately be terminated as a volunteer. That is not legal. That is in violation of a volunteer's First Amendment right of free speech.

As long as the information is true and not divulging personal information about another person, a volunteer has the right to speak freely to anyone about her observation and knowledge of the shelter, the animals, and the policies and procedures.

Banning photography and videotaping at the shelter

You have the right to video and photograph public places of the shelter to include the shelter conditions, animal care, and the animals to document your claims against the shelter, as well as to make efforts to find homes or rescues for the animals. These are forms of free speech. Moreover, you have the right to disseminate any images you own.

Many shelters ban citizens, and especially volunteers, from taking photographs and videotaping anything inside the shelter. This is illegal, because they are forms of expressing your first amendment right of free speech.

If your shelter bans photography and videotaping, tell them to have their attorney look up Animal Legal Defense Fund vs. Otter, 2014 WL 4388158*10 (D. Idaho 2014), and Alvarez, 679 F.3d 583, 597 (7th Cir. 2012), that ruled in favor of the citizens. Your free speech also extends to the right to disseminate your photographs and videos.

Also refer them to Section 1983. You might want to keep a small note of these with you when you go to the shelter to give to whoever denies you your rights.

Here is what the government officials, and you, need to know about Section 1983, per Nathan Winograd, No-Kill guru:

Section 1983

Here is an excerpt of an article by a well-respected attorney on the subject of 42 U.S.C. § 1983, or Section 1983:

There can be no dispute that complaining about abuses or violations of law at Shelters is a constitutionally protected right. A rescuer not only has the First Amendment right to speak out against abuses and violations of law committed by a governmental entity, he or she also has a constitutionally protected right to demand that the government correct the wrongs that are identified. This includes the right to threaten to sue or to actually file suit against the Shelter.

Government officials rarely admit that they have intentionally meted out punishment beyond the scope of their legal power; therefore, the law allows plaintiffs to use direct or circumstantial evidence to establish that punishing protected conduct was the government's motive in an action such as suspending adoption rights. Circumstantial evidence may include showing that the rescuer's privileges were withdrawn within a narrow time frame around the time he or she engaged in protected conduct, and that no other explanation or reason was given for the rescuer's punishment.

The last element of the Section 1983 claim, actual injury, can be demonstrated merely by showing that the rescuer has suffered a loss of any governmental benefit or privilege. It is important to emphasize that the loss of a common benefit counts as injury; a rescuer need not establish a legal right to adopt animals or take advantage of any other benefits afforded by a Shelter. As the Supreme Court has stated, a government entity "may not deny a benefit to a person on a basis that infringes his constitutionally protected interests—especially, his interest in freedom of speech." Therefore, it should be enough to show, for example, that a person has been deprived of his or her ability to volunteer at or to adopt animals from, a Shelter.

A question may arise as to whether a volunteer or rescuer needs to wait for a government official to follow through on a threat to retaliate before filing a claim under Section 1983 or whether a threat of retaliation alone is sufficient to trigger one. For example, some volunteers have been told by officials that publicly speaking about a Shelter will result in the volunteer being banned. Since the whole point of a Section 1983 retaliation claim is to prevent the "chilling"(discouragement) of constitutionally protected rights, it seems clear enough that a threat of retaliation for exercising those rights, which is specifically designed to obstruct the exercise of those rights, should be sufficient to satisfy the actual injury element of a Section 1983 claim.

There would be little hope of progress in improving the conditions at municipal animal Shelters if rescuers—the people likely most knowledgeable about those conditions—could be intimidated into remaining silent by the threat of retaliation. Thus, Section 1983 can be a powerful tool not only to obtain justice for people unfairly

treated by government officials, but also to insure that rescuers and animal Shelter reformers can continue their critically important work in saving lives and educating the public about our Shelter systems."
http://www.nathanwinograd.com

Chapter 3
Typical Threats

Animal control officers and the higher-ups who are the actual decision-makers for animal control policies have a common set of threats and tactics to try to get animal advocates to shut up and leave them alone. Here are some of them, and some possible ways you can respond to them.

First, the best response to any push-back is always, "We will not give up until the animals are safe, well cared for, and this shelter is no-kill." More than a response, this HAS to be your mission. Never give up. Make it your mantra. Your job is not done until you have fulfilled this mission.

If you try and then fizzle out, those in charge will be convinced that they have weathered the storm and that they are invincible. This will make it even more difficult for you to try again. Not impossible, but more difficult.

Here are some typical threats from those in charge:

- The more you complain (or if you go to the media, etc.), the worse it will get for the animals (implied or direct threat to kill more animals).

    Response:
    - How so, exactly?
    - We know for SURE more animals will suffer and be killed by the shelter in the future if we DON'T step up and demand reform, so this is a hollow threat. You're going to kill them anyway. And now we have you on record threatening to kill animals in retaliation for taxpayers speaking up about the conditions.

- We will let citizens know you have threatened to retaliate against the animals for us exercising our First Amendment rights to try to help them.

- You are interfering with government operations, so we are banning you from XXX.

  Response:
  - Specifically HOW am I interfering with government operations?
  - I am a citizen, and am protected by the First Amendment of the Constitution. If you ban me or have me arrested, you will be in violation of my First Amendment rights. You need to tell your attorney to look up Section 1983. We have a right to participate in our taxpayer-funded functions. This right has successfully been used in the courts against government actions just like this one you're threatening.
  - We will let citizens know that you consider our trying to help the shelter animals as interference.

- You are defaming us. We will sue you!

  Response:
  - Specifically how are we defaming you?
  - Do you understand that the ironclad defense to defamation is the truth? We are telling the truth. Just because it exposes the terrible conditions and kill rate at the shelter, doesn't make it defamatory.
  - Do you understand that defamation is damaging the GOOD reputation of something? Your reputation is one of

being a ruthless hellhole, death trap for animals under your care and control, so exposing that you EARNED your horrible reputation does no damage it.

- If you do that, do you understand that in discovery, you will have to first, tell the truth, and second, produce all the written records and documentation about the shelter for the world to see?
- The media will have a field day with this if you sue us, and we will see to it.
- Also, keep in mind that defamation goes both ways. If you do not tell the truth about US and harm our reputation, then YOU are defaming us.
- We will countersue you for malicious prosecution and violation of our First Amendment rights.
- We will let citizens know that you have threatened to sue us for trying to help and save the shelter's animals.

- You are a distraction. While we spend time with you, we could have been spending time with the animals.
  Response:
  - We wouldn't be here if you had been spending sufficient time with the animals. You need to get used to us, because we will continue to be here until this shelter is reformed.
  - If you would allow us to work together and let volunteers come into the shelter and help save these animals, this would not be a problem. It's a win/win situation. We can help save animals, and that means less work for you.

- We can't allow you in the pound, because it is a safety concern. We cannot risk someone getting hurt since we don't know these dogs.

> Response:
> - We are willing to sign a waiver of liability that will get you off the hook for our safety.
> - Why do you have a facility that is unsafe? There are thousands of other facilities that allow supervised interaction with the animals. It's not impossible.
> - Please provide us with a copy of your written policy on that.
> - We will let citizens know that you admit that you use their tax dollars to operate a shelter that is unsafe for people.

Be prepared to be threatened, but don't be intimidated. Be calm, be in control, and **document everything**. You are a taxpayer. You have rights. The shelter is a government-run department that should be run as professionally as any other department. Can you imagine being threatened if you complained about garbage collection? No. They have no right to threaten you, the animals, or your First Amendment rights.

Stand up for the animals. They depend on you.

Chapter 4
Beware of Unicorns and Rainbows

As you embark on your shelter reformation journey, be alert to all information that your shelter is releasing. As we have already discussed, changing the shelter will be a challenge, and those connected to the shelter and its operation will do everything they can to hinder your work. You will face denials, outright lies, deceit, and accusations; and you will have to be strong, stick to the facts, and challenge their opposition at every turn.

Don't let them get away with their lies and propaganda. Call them on it.

Typically, a kill shelter will do and say whatever it takes to present that they are a "happy place" for the unwanted dogs and cats. We call this the "Unicorns and Rainbows" effect. Shelter administration and their supporters will often outright lie and deny they kill healthy animals, stating that any animals they kill were sick or aggressive, when in fact they are killing healthy, adoptable animals for a myriad of convenient, trumped-up reasons.

Examining the records on each animal they choose to kill should show if the animal had medical or behavior issues, and if a veterinarian or behavioral specialist evaluated the animal's issue (in person) and judged that the animal MUST be euthanized.

Case in point: a shelter boasts that they are "*practically* no-kill" and that they find homes for ALL the animals brought in, when in fact their annual kill rate has been more than 40% for the last three years. FORTY PERCENT. However, the vast majority of the public does not know this percentage! They readily accept the statements and public posts on social media as the truth, and until your group exposes the lies and can back them up with the real facts, they will continue to believe that their shelter is all "unicorns and rainbows." It is up to YOU to maintain a steady, deliberate pressure to expose the truths and make the change.

Another myth that the public believes is if the shelter is a big, fancy building with smiling volunteers, it is the perfect place for unwanted animals and they obviously find homes for all of them. This again can be far from the truth! The size and appearance of the facility does not mean it is no-kill – not by a long shot.

Whatever the size of your shelter's building, it can and should be no-kill. We, along with many other dedicated and determined animal advocates, worked with a small city/county shelter that had a 75% plus kill rate and was operated out of a concrete block building with no back wall and only two large pens.

Today that same shelter operates out of that same building, which now is completely enclosed with separate indoor and outdoor runs and a play yard, and boasts a less than 1% kill rate. To compare, the large shelter mentioned in the previous paragraph has a two million dollar facility and is still a high-kill shelter.

Make the facts and stats known to the citizens. The real numbers will have a huge impact on your ability to gather public support to make the change!

Chapter 5
Your Battle Plan

Your first approach to reforming the shelter should be to try to work *with* the people in charge. They have the capability of enacting change, so if you can work with them, partner with them, that is by far the preferred route.

First, offer your help and give it when allowed. You can tell them that you understand that taking care of animals is a lot of work, and you are willing to help them do it.

To that end, you have to let them know exactly what you can offer to improve the shelter, and that it will cost them nothing. That's a plus for them.

Offer assistance

What can your group offer? Your help should not be offered *in lieu* of reform, but rather to mitigate the problems while reform is enacted. It is a not a swap. You still insist on reform, but in the interim, you want to help the shelter employees do their job and improve the lives of the animals.

They may make you sign a Volunteer Agreement, which is fine. Keep a copy of it, though.

A primary advantage to offering to help is that more animals will be treated better by your mere presence and hands-on help. Another advantage is that by gaining the trust of the people in the shelter and those in charge, as you push for real reform, they already know and respect you and your opinion. And finally, by being in and around the shelter, you get an inside look at how they do business. The more supporters you have in the inside, the better.

Here are some ways you can offer to help:

- Feeding the animals – making sure they are fed, the bowls are cleaned and sanitized, and that everyone is getting enough food.
- Cleaning – yes, poop scooping. It's important to the health and wellbeing of the animals. The ACOs hate doing it, so they often simply don't. By offering, you improve the conditions and health of the animals and befriend the ACOs.

- Being aware of illness or injury to the animals and reporting it to someone who can help the animal.
- Caring for animals that need special attention such as pregnant, elderly, or recovering animals.
- Grooming and bathing animals.
- Giving flea and tick treatments.
- Socializing the animals and giving play time and exercise so they are less apt to develop kennel anxiety.
- Observing and documenting each animal's behavior and temperament.
- Teaching animals basic commands, and training out bad behaviors, which makes them more adoptable.
- Making repairs or improvements to the facilities.
- Finding in-kind donations of things the shelter needs.
- Networking the animals on PetFinder, Facebook, and other networking sites.
- Writing grants for the shelter.
- Following up on spay and neuter agreements.
- Transporting animals to and from the vet.

The reality

The reality, however, is often that they don't want your help. They think everything is fine and don't accept your offers to help improve the shelter. And, honestly, if they really wanted something changed, they had to power to do it already and haven't, so that tells you all you need to know.

If they turn you down, or even throw you an ineffectual crumb to make you shut up, then you have to take a different approach. You must FORCE reform.

If you want to win a war – and make no mistake, this will be a **war** – you must have a battle plan. To go into such an important and protracted battle, flying by ass-on-fire, only reacting to whatever crisis is before you, will be a waste of time and energy.

You must have a battle plan. Write it down. Share it with your group members, but NOT with the opposition, at least not all at once.

Your army

Start with your core group, your army. Don't be discouraged if you are the only one in your group at first. People are reluctant for many valid reasons to go openly against people in power. Making enemies, especially in small towns, is a risky thing. Plus, being an activist entails some amount of instant aversion among those who don't do such things. You will be labeled a troublemaker, a rabble-rouser, a pain in the ass, and just plain crazy, especially by those who you will confront while bringing about reform.

You probably already know who your friends are, who has guts and good ideas, and who will stand beside you in this war no matter what. Those people are your core group.

Then determine who in your core group does what well. Leverage your strengths. If one of you has PR, writing, or media experience, that person should head up those activities. If someone has organizing activities, have that person do event planning. You get the picture.

But the more you are able to divvy up duties, the less overwhelmed you all will be. If you are an army of one, then your plan is even more important, because you will have to pace yourself and plan cautiously so you can keep moving forward without becoming burned out.

As you get farther down the road, you may have other people who want to help. That's great, but be sure you know their motives are pure. It is not beyond reason that your opposition will send someone to infiltrate your group. Not likely, but possible. So, before letting down your guard, check them out. Look at their social media, check with their vet, and ask if anyone you know can vouch for them. Then determine what they bring to the table. What are their strengths? What do they want to do? What are their time constraints? Then you can figure out how best they fit in.

On the flip side, if you have a specific need and know someone who fits that niche and you see that they are an animal lover, you may want to enlist their help. Such people may include attorneys, graphic artists, event planners, media pros, etc.

Here are some activities you will need someone to perform:

- Social media upkeep – this must be ongoing and current.
- Spokesperson – this person is the face of the group. She should be THE one person who talks with media, giving official statements and interviews. The spokesperson should also go before government meetings during citizen input sessions. She should be the one to officially present proposals, demands, etc. to government officials.
- Media – someone to write press releases and talk to media. She must be able to go on-air and talk in a calm, concise manner. She must write press releases to let media know of events, and when someone from the group will appear before government meetings. This person may also take photos and video to disseminate to your followers and media.
- Event planning – someone must do logistics of protests and events, including obtaining necessary permits, signage, badges, coordination, tables, printed matter, water, etc.
- Administration – this person will maintain databases of followers, media, government officials, donors, etc. This person, or someone else who is an excellent writer, should be able to write, compile, and disseminate the Freedom of Information Act requests, and then follow up on them, which may include showing up to visibly view and/or copy the provided documents.
- Legal advice – having someone to bounce questions off of can be helpful, especially if

you think there may be legal wrongdoing by the pound or the government.

- Number crunching – someone who knows how to crunch numbers will be invaluable. This person can sift through piles of stats, invoices, reports, budgets, spreadsheets, etc., and come up with hard data that can be used to support your efforts.
- Mole – if possible, having someone who is unknown to the shelter officials and not openly affiliated with your group to go into the shelter as a worker or volunteer – a mole – can be very helpful. They can gather information to help you further your reform efforts.

Documentation

Documentation is your proof that supports your allegations of wrongdoing at a shelter. You need documentation before you make assumptions and allegations, or you run the risk of defamation. Randomly and wildly claiming that a shelter or a shelter employee is cruel or breaking the law can get you in legal hot water. You need to be truthful and accurate, and able to provide evidence of allegations of wrongdoing to force change.

Some documents may be easier to obtain than others, but they are critical, even if you have to get them via a Freedom of Information Act (FOIA) request. See the chapter on FOIAs for more information.

Here are documents you need to obtain as quickly as possible:

- Copy of Section 1983. You can find this on Google and then print it out. You may need to keep a lot of copies of this available to educate the people who are in charge of the shelter.
- State laws related to animals, especially cruelty, abuse, and funding. These are often found online.

- Local ordinances and statutes related to animals, including abuse, neglect, fighting, vaccinations, leash laws, breed-specific bans, fees, stray hold times, spay and neuter, funding for spay/neuter, regulations, insurance, registration, license fees, etc. These may be found online.
- The official shelter policy and procedures manual. They may not have one or claim that they do not have one. If they do not, force them to put that claim in writing in case you have to bring a lawsuit against them. You may have to get it or make them deny having one using a FOIA.
- Specific policy on how the shelter determines which animals are unadoptable and therefore can be killed.
- Job descriptions and requirements (certifications) for everyone who works at the shelter, including volunteers.
- Documentation of certifications and education/training of shelter employees, especially if they are noted as part of a job description or take part in killing animals.
- Proof of ongoing education and training of shelter employees.
- Vehicle log miles monthly reports for the last three years. These show how many miles the Animal Control Officers traveled and where.
- The mission statement of any animal control or animal shelter government committee.
- The minutes from each meeting of the animal control committee for the past three years.
- Full city or county budgets (whichever funds the animal shelter) for the last three years, making sure that the line item income and expenses (budgeted and actual) for the shelter are shown.

- Copies of invoices (not receipts – INVOICES that note each service provided) from the shelter veterinarians who have anything to do with the care, guidance, or euthanization of animals for the last three years.
- The city or county policy (whichever pays the shelter employees) and procedures for hiring and firing employees.
- The shelter's official monthly reports showing live-release percentage, intake and disposition, specifically actual numbers of intakes, adoptions, returns to owner (RTO), kills, escapes, death by illness or injury, in-shelter births, missing, quarantines, legal holds, hoarding, seizures, transfer to rescues or another facility, and running count of animals for the last three years.

Reform Plan

Your Reform Plan is the document that will guide you through your reform process. You must know what you want, to get it. Beating your chest and screaming vague, unsubstantiated problems you claim about the shelter will get you absolutely nowhere, and will, in fact, set back the process.

Your reform demands must be specific, justifiable, and realistic. And, yes, despite what they will claim at the top of their lungs, no-kill is realistic. Changes will have to be made, but no-kill **IS** realistic.

Have someone who writes well or professionally create your Reform Plan. It should be professional and easy to comprehend. It should include support information, as well as budgets, laws, etc.

Here's an example of a reform plan:

Reform Plan for the XXXX Animal Shelter
Presented by the Reform XXXX Group

The XXXX Animal Shelter is the agency that is used by the City of XXXX to manage animal control. It is directly managed by the XXX Police Department and employs two Animal Control Officers (ACOs).

As a taxpayer-funded agency, taxpayers demand quality services from the shelter, just as we demand quality services from other government services such as police protection, fire protection, and garbage pick-up.

Official shelter records from 2014 – 2017 show that the shelter has had custody and control of XXXX animals, and has a live-release rate of just XX%. The flip side of that horrific number is that XX% of the animals in the custody and control of the shelter never make it out alive.

Taxpayers deserve better service than that. We would not stand for the police, fire, or garbage departments being successful at their job only XX% of the time, and we do not accept that abysmal success rate from the shelter.

A walk through the shelter shows a facility that is in great disrepair, unsanitary, not climate controlled for the health and comfort of the animals, and kennels that are overcrowded, which leads to the spread of diseases, pregnancies, and injuries from fighting.

A review of state animal control laws requires that all animals, even those in the custody of government agencies, must be housed in humane, safe conditions, and have adequate shelter, food, and water. While laws dictate the bare minimum conditions for animals, common decency dictates that since animals are sentient beings, they should be treated with more than the most basic of care.

Furthermore, since the shelter picks up homeless and stray animals, they often acquire family pets, which then suffer under the conditions and maltreatment at the shelter, and only have a XX% chance of making it out alive. These "euthanized" animals could have been an elderly person's companion animal, a child's pet, or beloved by a heartbroken family.

Finally, the conditions and policies of the shelter are bad business for our community. Economic development depends upon having a location that is satisfactory for businesses to create and transport their products, AND that is a family-friendly environment for their employees. When companies evaluate sites to locate or relocate businesses, they take into account how responsive and accommodating a government is to its citizens.

Sixty-eight percent of America's families have pets and most of the remainder love animals. A "shelter" that murders XX% of the animals that come into it, shows a disregard for family values, a shelter that is not professionally managed, and mismanagement of taxpayer funds by the government.

The converse, and selling points to site selectors, are a no-kill animal shelter, spay and neuter programs, and dog parks.

For these and so many more reasons, we demand the reform of the XXX Shelter.

Reform requirements
No-Kill

- Increase of the live-release rate to 95% or more within six months.
- Good faith, concerted effort to partner with rescue groups to transfer appropriate animals if they have not been adopted within two weeks after their stray hold.
- Aggressive effort to network and market the animals for adoption through PetFinder, expanded shelter visitation times, and local adoption events.

Policies and procedures

- A policy that does not allow an animal to be euthanized because of alleged behavioral problems until it has been objectively evaluated by an outside behavioral specialist, the behaviors documented, and a report made.
- A policy that if an adopter or rescue makes a commitment on an animal, the animal will not be killed.
- A policy that separates male and females in gang pens.
- A policy that provides parvo and other vaccinations, de-wormer, and flea and tick control to every animal within six hours of intake, and records of such being kept on each animal.
- If the voucher procedure for spay or neuter is used, you must follow up closely after the allotted time period to see if the voucher has been used, then follow up with people who have not complied with the voucher.
- Public dissemination of the pound's monthly statistics showing intake numbers, release numbers, kill rate, number of kills, adoptions, rescues, return-to-owners, death, and escapes.
- A policy allowing volunteers to come into the shelter and assist in the care and networking of the animals.

Facility

- The facility must be environmentally controlled such that all animals are housed between 60 – 80 degrees at all times, and

have shelter from the wind, direct sunshine, and rain.
- A policy with no more than four (compatible) adult animals per kennel.
- A policy that mandates best standards for infection control and sanitation.

———— ———— ———— ————

This example is just a starting point. You must customize it to make it fit your shelter's needs. Remember to support your conclusions with statistics, explain why the reforms are important to citizens AND voters, and the up-side to the reforms for the government.

Have copies of your Reform Plan for the XXXX Shelter printed and available in case you run into a supporter or detractors and have an opportunity to educate them. Also post it online for citizens to get behind and share.

Also have copies of it for every member of the committees or councils when you speak to them about reforming the shelter.

Chapter 6
Crunching Government Numbers

You have a right to know what your government-run shelter is doing, so that means you need numbers. Numbers will show the reality versus the spin.

Numbers will show how the shelter is performing. Numbers give you a foundation to inquire why a tax-payer facility that has a kill rate of, say, sixty percent, is only successful forty percent of the time. As a citizen, you would not accept other government-run agencies such as the police, fire department or even garbage collection to do their job only forty percent of the time.

Your tax dollars fund Animal Control, and therefore they must use your tax dollars to maintain a high standard of service. Murdering sixty percent of the animals that come into their control and custody is not a high standard of service.

Official numbers, provided by government entities supposedly show what they are doing with taxpayer dollars. Granted, they can manipulate those numbers, but if you can prove it they did, someone will be in BIG trouble.

You need to obtain every set of reports and statistics that exist about your shelter. Sometimes you can just ask your local government representative (city council person or county commissioner), or the city or county clerk's office for these and they will provide them to you.

But, sometimes, you have to obtain these by a Freedom of Information Act (FOIA) request.

Either way, get them.

Once you have them, crunch the numbers. If someone on your team is an Excel spreadsheet guru, this would be a great job for them. If you don't have an Excel guru, that's okay. You don't have to be a statistician to know when something doesn't add up.

These numbers will help you prove to your government officials, in a factual, unbiased way, what is going on in the shelter and what needs improvement.

For instance, if the kill rate for your shelter was 98% in the years before your volunteer group started helping, and now it's 50%, it proves that your group not only saves lives, but saves the government money, as well. The logical conclusion is, therefore, that it is in the shelter's best fiscal interest, and a better management of taxpayer dollars, to further allow or to assist your volunteer group in finding homes or rescues for the animals.

To follow are some numbers you want to crunch and what you're looking for.

Official Monthly and Yearly Shelter Reports

See Chapter 7 - Analyzing Shelter Numbers.

Shelter Budget

The budget will tell you important things such as how much taxpayer money the shelter has to work with and how it is spent.

Get the line item budgets for the last three or so years.

Look for:

- Revenue sources. What revenue does the shelter generate from adoption, rescue, and owner-return fees? Does any revenue come from other sources such as the general fund, grants, fundraisers, or donations?
- Revenue versus actual expenses.
- Money budgeted versus actual money spent in each line item.
- What happened to the previous years' surpluses (if any)? Were they kept in the shelter budget or were they transferred to another budget line?
- Allocations for capital improvements (building expansion, equipment, etc.).

- Allocations for employees. Did they fill empty positions? If not, where did the funds for the position go?
- Building maintenance and repairs. Did they have funds and not use them?
- Expenses for the shelter vet including sufficient and types of euthanization drugs.
- The cost of each euthanization.
- Expenses for animal care and feeding supplies.
- Sufficient purchase of food, flea and tick treatments, infection control, and sanitation supplies.
- Contributions to and use of any law-mandated funds like spay and neuter programs.
- Anything else that impacts the shelter's ability to care for the animals.

Shelter Veterinarian Invoices

Your shelter vet bills the government that runs the shelter for their services and supplies associated with the shelter. You want to see those numbers. Here's what you're looking for:

- Amount billed per month and per year for the last three years.
- Does that annual amount require that the vet service be bid out? If so, was it?
- Go through each invoice individually and look for the fees for euthanasia. In most states, the vet must list the date of euthanization and the identification of the animal. Many states require the vet to note the method of euthanization.
- Compare dates of specific euthanizations with the intake date on animals to ensure that the shelter adhered to the mandatory waiting period in your state.

- Compare the identification number of the animal euthanized to the shelter record of the disposition of that animal.
- Compare services for an animal with the shelter's documentation of that animal. For instance, if a vet spays or neuters an animal, compare that bill with the animal's record. Or if an animal is shown by the shelter to be ill or injured and had to be euthanized, see if that is corroborated with the vet's invoice for that date.
- If an animal was injured or gives birth while in the shelter, verify that it was given the proper medical attention by the vet bill.
- Determine the cost of each euthanization. Multiply the cost per the number of animals euthanized annually. Compare that number, which is an expense, to the money that would be revenue if those animals had been adopted (for a fee) or rescued. Use this number to show that killing is not only unnecessary, but poor money management.
- Compare the costs of the charge by the vet to spay or neuter an animal, versus what the shelter charges for adoptions to see the difference.
- Did they charge for baths and grooming? If so, why couldn't the shelter have volunteers do this and save money?
- Did they have a charge for disposing of deceased animals' bodies? If so, did they pay a service for this? Some shady vets simply dump the bodies in the garbage cans on garbage collection days and pocket the disposal charge.

If you come across discrepancies in the numbers, ask for an explanation in writing and let your supporters know what you're doing. Then keep documenting the process to keep a record of their responses. If there appears to be financial mishandling, contact your state comptroller in writing and ask for an audit, specifically listing your concerns.

Shelter reform must be argued on FACTS. Government officials are interested in money, public relations, the law, and risk management. The very act of asking for the records will let the people in charge know that you mean business, that you know what you're doing, and you have a plan. Keep this in mind as you analyze the numbers.

Chapter 7
Analyzing Shelter Numbers

Most states require that your shelter keep certain records and to create reports since they are a government agency. This information is public and subject to the scrutiny of citizens.

You may ask your city or county clerk for those records and hope they give them to you. If they refuse, use a Freedom of Information Act (FOIA) Request to obtain them.

Shelter Intake Forms and animal records are supposed to provide the complete history of every animal that comes into the control and custody of the shelter. These are invaluable in making sure that the shelter is abiding by animal welfare laws.

Live-release percentage

Of course, the most important statistic is the live-release percentage, or in the case of hellhole "shelters", the kill percentage. This rate should be noted or easily calculated from the shelter's monthly and annual reports.

Shelters claim they "euthanize" animals for good reasons. Right off the bat, there's a problem. According to the Iowa State College of Veterinary Medicine, euthanasia is "a moral obligation to ensure the welfare of animals. Therefore, when disease or injury conditions arise that diminish quality of life or create pain and suffering that cannot be effectively relieved by medical means..." an animal should be euthanized.

Killing an animal for any other reason is NOT euthanasia. It's murder.

Shelters kill animals for reasons they certainly won't tell you. Here are some:

- Space – the shelter is crowded, because they make little or no effort to find adopters or rescues for the animals. Crowded shelters cost food, are time-consuming, create dangerous situations for the animals and workers, and are a lot of work. So it's easier to kill animals than to do the right thing and find homes or rescues for them.
- Disease outbreak – parvo, distemper, and upper respiratory infections are highly contagious and can be deadly. They WILL tell you about this rationale for mass murdering all the animals in the shelter, but it's still deceptive. The worse a shelter's infection control and sanitation practices, the more likely they will experience disease outbreaks. Poorly run, lazy shelter personnel will choose to kill all the animals, claim it is the humane thing to do, and then claim they had to do it so they could do deep cleaning. But, they do not HAVE to kill every animal in the shelter. Professionally run shelters have a protocol to quarantine animals, watch them for signs of disease, treat ones that are ill, and make a case-by-case decision on euthanasia.
- Overt or covert breed bias – some shelters routinely kill Pit Bulls just because they are Pit Bulls, or at least they think so. They often don't know a Pit Bull from any other dog that happens to have a sort of wide muzzle, or a similar Pit look. They will label a

possible Pit Bull "unadoptable" without further explanation or authoritative documentation to support their death sentence.

- Lazy Animal Control Officer (ACO) – he or she doesn't like feeding, picking up poop, sanitizing, and dealing with the animals.
- Weekend or holiday – often ACOs are on call weekends and holidays and must only come to the shelter for bare-bones maintenance. The fewer animals, the less time they have to spend there.

For these reasons and more, you need to scrutinize each animal's Intake Form and then compare and verify the animal's disposition (outcome) as well as the shelter's overall numbers.

Here are some numbers you're looking for and why:

Intake Form information

Each shelter should have a separate form on every animal. This form usually lists:

- Date of intake
- Animal ID number
- Place of intake
- Time of intake
- Type of intake – stray, owner surrender, left at shelter, court case, quarantine
- Type of animal – dog/cat/rabbit
- ACO
- Gender of animal
- Breed
- Approximate age
- Approximate size
- Spayed/neutered

- Collar and/or tags
- Micro-chip
- Owner release signature and information
- Animal condition
- Vaccination/medical information
- Disposition
- Returned to owner date
- Adopted date
- Rescued date
- Missing /escaped date
- Died in custody date
- Euthanized date
- Signature and information about owner, adopter, or rescue organization.

What you want to know

Insure that all **animal ID numbers** are accounted for and matched with intake sheets. If intakes are numbered numerically, check to see that every number has a corresponding intake form and that no numbers are skipped. For instance, if they are numbered consecutively starting at the first of the year, find intake forms for each number. If a number is missing, you want to know the reason and to see corresponding documentation about what happened to that animal.

This is important to ensure:
- Animals are being held for the mandatory stray period of time to allow owners to reclaim their pet. If an animal had a collar when picked up, one should assume it is a lost pet.
- Animals are accurately listed as either a stray, owner surrender, or court case. The difference can be life or death. Owner

surrenders can be killed as soon as they walk through the door, since there is no potential owner looking for them.

- Animals are not being picked up by ACOs and sold or given away to anyone, but especially for fighting, reselling, bunching, or breeding purposes.
- ACOs are intentionally not listing animals that they pick up so they can flip (sell) the animals. This happens with animals that appear to be pure-bred.
- All animals are being listed publicly so their owners can be reunited with them or so they can be adopted or rescued.
- Animals are not being secretly killed, or not listed and then killed.
- Animals are not being euthanized because of their mistreatment or injury while in the custody and control of the shelter.
- Animals don't inadvertently drop through the cracks and reach their kill date without being networked for RTO, adoption, or rescue.

Date of intake

Analyze:

- If animals are kept the mandatory hold period before being killed. Compare the shelter vet's invoices billing for euth fees with each animal's intake date and disposition date.
- How long it takes from intake until an animal is listed on PetFinder or otherwise made known and available to be reunited with its owner, or marketed and networked for adoption or rescue.

Animal Control Officers (ACOs)

- Does an ACO seem to be overly aggressive in locating animals or a certain breed of animal?
- Does an ACO seem to have a worse euthanization rate than another?
- Do the animals picked up by certain ACOs seem to go missing or escape more than another?
- Do more animals picked up by one ACO seem to be injured than those of another ACO?
- Does one ACO seem to deem more animals as aggressive?
- If there is more than one ACO, and they swap off the authority to have an animal euthanized, are more animals killed under one ACO's authorization than another?

Breed

- Look for any trends involving the intake, descriptions, temperament, and disposition of a specific breed such as Pit Bull. Are they automatically noted as aggressive?
- Are certain breeds euthanized quicker than other breeds, i.e. Pit Bulls.
- Verify that animals that appear to be purebreds go to rescues or adopters instead of mysteriously disappearing or shown as euthanized, but the vet has no record of the euth.

Owner release

- If an owner releases an animal, there is a place on the form where they sign, as well as a question about if they want to be notified before the animal is euthanized. If they sign that they do, and the animal was euthanized, was the owner contacted beforehand?

- Does the owner give information about the animal such as if it is good around children, has no behavior problems, etc., but the animal was never given an opportunity to be networked and euthanized anyway?

Adopted date and adopter
- Are there any trends that specific individuals seem to be adopting a lot of animals, especially Pit Bulls or purebreds?
- If your shelter does not spay/neuter before release, do they follow up in the allotted amount of time to ensure that the animal is spayed or neutered to ensure that they are not being used for breeding purposes or used for bait or fighting?

Missing/escaped date
- Animals should not just disappear from a shelter. Period. They are responsible for documenting the disposition (end result) of all animals that come into their control and custody.
- Match all available records on any missing/escaped animals to ensure that they all tell the same story.
- Make sure that missing/escaped animals aren't on the shelter vet's euth invoice for that month.
- Do the missing/escaped animals have any patterns such as during one ACO's watch or before a holiday?
- Are the missing/escaped animals purebreds, Pit Bulls, or possible fighting bait animals? Young animals (puppies and kittens), frail animals, timid and elderly animals, and even bunnies are all at risk to be used as bait to train fighting dogs.

Died in custody date

- Match all available records on these animals to ensure that they are all tell the same story.
- Was there documentation of any illness or injury to the animal before its death?
- Make sure that they aren't on the shelter vet's euth invoice for that month.
- Do these animals have any patterns such as during one ACO's watch or before a holiday?
- Are they purebreds, or Pit Bulls, or possible fighting bait animals?

Euthanized date

- Were the animals kept the mandatory hold period before being killed?
- Why were they killed? If overcrowding, was the shelter really overcrowded?
- Were they deemed aggressive? Why? Who deemed them as such? What is the policy on determining aggression?
- Were they made available and known to the public so they could be reunited with their owners or given an opportunity to be networked/marketed to save their lives?
- Are there any patterns in the euthanizations such as breeds, ACOs, before holidays, etc.?

The final disposition

As heartbreaking as it is, you need to compare the number and timing of animals they claim to have euthanized with the corresponding euth invoice from the veterinarian who did it, IF they use a vet. Then, you might want to see how the bodies of the animals were disposed. We found that one shelter vet did all killing before noon on a certain day of the week, because that day happened to be garbage pick-up day. He saved money by dumping the deceased animals in the garbage rather than having a disposal service handle them. Check your state animal disposal laws to see if the vet adhered to them.

This is a LOT of work. I know firsthand, because I've done it. But, but having the numbers in front of you, you can provide solid, factual, provable information to your government officials about what needs changing or what can be improved at your shelter.

If they don't work with you, then the media might find the numbers very interesting and do an investigation of the shelter. If something appears suspicious, you can use the information to request an audit by the State Comptroller.

Chapter 8
Get Their Attention

To reform a shelter, you have to first get the attention of the people who have the power to enact change: government officials.

They have a lot of people clambering for their attention, trying to carve out a piece of their time, and possibly grab some budget money. The last thing they want to hear from are some bleeding-heart, crazy dog women whining about how heartless they are, how animals are suffering because of it, and that they have blood on their hands.

Frankly, they may be heartless, but they sure don't want to be told that. It's not a good conversation opener.

Or, it may be that they have not had reason to really think about the shelter in depth. It may be just one of those things that falls through the cracks. Unless something unusual gets their attention, they just don't think about it.

Face it, if they had wanted better conditions at the shelter and to save more animals, they would have already put policies to do that in place. There surely have been people who have screamed bloody murder off and on for years about the shelter, and they have given up before forcing change, so if the people in power have given it some thought; they now just dismiss any attempts at reform as yet another futile annoyance that will soon pass like all the other attempts. That's why THIS time, you don't stop until you succeed.

Your mission is to make shelter reform something worth their thinking about, again. You have to get government officials' attention, but it has to be the people who can make change.

Usually, shelter employees can't make policy changes. Anything of importance has to be approved by someone higher up in the hierarchy. There may be a flow chart showing something like this:

- **County and/or City Mayor (sometimes called a City Manager)** – They are usually held to the decisions of the County Commission or City Council, but ultimately they often get their way. They are concerned about how the public views them and the city and county, because keeping their jobs depends on it. They are susceptible to media pressure, public protests, and citizens voicing concerns. You need to get them on your side.
- **County Commission and/or City Council** –They are supposed to serve the people in their specific district they represent. They get to vote on resolutions and action items. You need to influence them.
- **Police Department or Sheriff's Office** – They often handle Animal Control responsibilities, because they are the law enforcement agencies of local government. Shelter employees, especially the Animal Control Officers (ACOs) report directly to the Police Chief or Sheriff. The ACOs may be deputized so they can write citations and arrest people who have broken local laws.

  Even if they don't exactly figure in the authority hierarchy, you need to have them on your side, especially if you have Breed Specific Laws (BSLs) such as Pit Bull bans, which are often used as excuses to allow shelters to kill animals under the guise of being "aggressive." They need to be informed about the facts of BSLs and how they are bogus and create a risk of lawsuits.
- **City and county attorneys** – They interpret local laws, and ordinances, and state and federal laws. They also usually are called upon to assess risk management

including potential for lawsuits for shelter policies and procedures.

- **Animal Control Board** – This is the advisory board for the higher-ups. They depend upon them to consider and offer ideas and solutions to shelter policies and procedures. The board is usually comprised of a mix of people from the commissions and council people, law enforcement, veterinarian, and, if you're lucky, citizens and animal rights activists.

  The theory is that they are a broad, knowledgeable, objective guidance committee that can sift through information and come up with the very best answer to every shelter question. That is often not true. It is often political in nature and often serves to benefit those on the board somehow. Nonetheless, their input to the higher-ups is usually THE WORD and enacted.

  So, like it or not, you must influence this board to do the right thing. You must educate them and show them how what you want done is best for the city and county.

  Don't think that screaming about them being heartless or ignorant will have a positive effect on their decisions. It won't. You must try to work WITH them and spoon feed them information that they can give to the higher-ups and look like geniuses.

- **Animal Control Veterinarian** – The vet makes the decisions on policies about killing, aggressive animals, disease control, spay/neuter, humane sheltering, shelter climate control, vaccinations, and anything else that involves health and wellness of the animals.

They sometimes will make decisions or echo agreement with decisions made by non-medical higher-ups just to make things easier and to keep the paychecks flowing.

For instance, they are paid for every animal they kill, so deciding to SAVE as many as possible is not in their best financial interest. They may be quick to advise to kill all animals when there is a disease outbreak, rather than manage it. They may decide that some animals are too old, sick, or aggressive, so they recommend they be killed.

Sure, they can do things better, they can choose how they treat the animals and volunteers, and they can make or break a shelter, but only policies and laws can create permanent change.

So what gets government's attention?

- Laws
- Lawsuits
- Money
- Risk management
- Publicity
- Voters
- Their own jobs

Laws

Government is the embodiment of laws. It exists because of laws. Government officials supposedly rule according to laws. They are supposed to enforce laws, even if they don't like them. It's your job to educate them about animal welfare laws, to demand that they abide by them, and to be the watchdog to ensure their compliance.

Lawsuits

Government entities hate lawsuits. They are part of a big pool that handles their legal claims, so it's not necessarily the cost of litigation that gets to them. It's that when they draw lawsuit after lawsuit, their premium for that legal pool is increased.

Plus, it ties up government officials for things like depositions and testimony.

And, lawsuits are public information. It's up to you to make sure that the public – citizens and media – know about it.

Money

If people employed by the government, at any level, do anything fishy with the money, that's big trouble. Crunch the numbers and follow the money trail to be on the lookout for irregularities:

- Opportunity for someone to pocket money.
- Opportunities for someone to make money or receive gifts or compensation of any kind due to their position.
- Missing money.
- Possible kickbacks.
- Mismanagement.

Risk management

Risk management is how governments avoid lawsuits. Here are some issues that will get their attention:

- Breaking the law.
- Animal control laws.
- Animal cruelty laws.
- Killing of healthy, adoptable animals.
- Killing someone's known pet.
- Money irregularities.
- Contracts or purchases circumventing the bidding process.

- First Amendment (right to free speech) violations.
- Conflicts of interest.
- Abuse of power or authority.
- Lack of certifications or licenses.
- Fiscal mismanagement.
- Kickbacks to shelter employees, shelter vet, or government officials.
- Insider contracts to favored people, groups, or entities.
- Shelter employees selling shelter animals (especially purebreds), and selling animals for dog fighting, lab experiments, etc.
- Shelter employees pocketing fees.
- Dangerous conditions for citizens or employees at the shelter.
- Dangerous conditions for the citizens created by a shelter employee's driving or other employment-related actions.

Publicity

Publicity, both good and bad, is a motivator for government entities. They all want to appear as good public servants to their constituents. It makes their jobs easier and, if they are in an elected position, it helps their potential for re-election.

Publicity also has measurable economic impact, as well. At any given time, hundreds of companies are seeking locations to build or relocate. Your economic development director's job is to lure them to your city or county.

In their decision-making equation, companies factor in quality of life issues for their employees. Media reports are picked up by aggregation websites and become viral pretty quickly for someone interested in a particular city to review. They check not only official propaganda provided by the government, but they also review social websites. They Google for insider scoops.

They look at local and area newspapers and media reports. And they even consider things like travel rating sites.

A responsive, citizen-centric, compassionate governing body is far more appealing to a company's work force than one that ignores its citizens, a shelter that kills healthy animals and family pets, and mismanages its money.

So, your job is to know when and how to use publicity to your shelter reform mission's advantage. It's a powerful tool, so use it wisely.

Voters

Elected officials get their positions by supposedly representing the wishes of their constituency. Whenever possible, they like to assist their constituency in making things happen.

First, elect people who are sensitive to, and actually take concrete action on animal issues. Before elections, send out a poll to candidates about animal issues, and publicize their responses.

A state representative, congressperson, or senator has no direct power over a local government, but they can pressure them.

Ask your elected officials to help you. Ask them point blank to intervene. Ask them to make a phone call and ask your shelter to do whatever it is you need them to do. Ask them for a specific action, not just a listen.

When they do something, make sure that you let people know what they did – good or bad. Post it on your Facebook page. Send a press release. Make it public. If they helped, thank them publicly. If they ignored you, shame them publicly.

For more information about how to leverage elections to impact animal welfare, read the chapter Election Time.

Chapter 9
Freedom of Information Act Requests

A Freedom of Information Act (FOIA) request may be the single best tool for reforming government animal control facilities. The media runs a close second, but this is a very important tool. A FOIA request gives regular citizens access to government records and information. You are a taxpayer, so your dollars fund your local government and its programs and facilities including animal control and the pound.

If you intend to reform your local pound, you need to have facts. Screaming like a banshee to your local officials or media doesn't give you credibility; having accurate facts and figures does.

When possible, find open-source, public information. Most state laws, and city and county ordinances are readily available online. Research search engines, and ask your local librarian for help in uncovering records and public information. What you cannot locate elsewhere, you can request from the government, first informally, then, if necessary, formally via a FOIA request.

Governments are often loathe to voluntarily turn over their records and information to citizens, and even more so if they think you will use it against them and how they do business. But no matter how much of a fight they mount and how they try to dissuade you, you have a RIGHT to look at and even copy their records. Don't let them bluff you or bully you out of it.

First, ask in writing to the appropriate entity if you can view the records you want. Be specific. You do not have to tell them why you want them, nor do you have to justify wanting them. If you ask to have them copy records for you, expect to pay about a dollar or more per page for it, plus for their time doing it. That's why you might want to ask to view them and you either copy them (take your own scanner or copier) or take copious notes. Check out your specific state's Open

Records Act laws to see if they have a set allowable fee and more details about your state's requirements.

They might say they will charge you for the time they spend researching and pulling the records. They probably can't do that. Since you do not have access to them, and they are required by law to provide them, they are on the hook for making them accessible to you. But, just to be sure, check your state's laws or an attorney before raising a stink about it.

So, let's assume that a shelter or the city or county refuses or makes excuses to keep from providing you with records you want. That's when you submit a FOIA request. By doing this, they MUST respond in a timely manner and in good faith. It also puts them on notice that you know your rights and that you are serious about your goal.

FOIA requests are often reviewed by their in-house attorney, because they want to know if they have to respond, and they want to know what they can avoid disclosing. But that's a good thing. Attorneys understand that FOIAs must be answered and will usually tell the people in charge to follow through and make it happen.

Don't expect for them to make this pleasant for you. Some will, some won't, but they must reply in good faith. Document your process in case you have to refer back to it: Date, time, what you asked, what they did, etc.

You must also act in good faith. Here are some tips:

- Be polite and professional. Do not be adversarial. This is simply a business request. It's not the time to try to take anyone to task for anything.
- Be reasonable. Don't ask for things they don't have or cannot release. If they do not have what you are requesting, tell them what you are trying to find out and ask if they have

any records that would be able to give you that information.

- Request the most important data first.
- Don't request huge volumes of records in a single FOIA request. This is cumbersome, time-consuming, and confusing for them to compile all at once. Voluminous requests give them a reason to deny your request and delay the process.
- Technically, there is no limit to the FOIA requests you can submit, so ask for different types of records in separate FOIA requests. For instance, ask for all budget records and invoices in one request, the shelter intake records in another, and shelter policies and procedures in another. But beware, local officials often get very angry at FOIAs. After a couple of requests, they become less and less forthcoming. They might intentionally slow-walk the request into oblivion.
- Be very specific as to what records you want. Don't just request all records pertaining to the shelter. That is too vague and cumbersome. Ask for a specific set of records during a specific period of time such as veterinary services invoices from years 2012, 2013, 2014, and year to date.
- Be open to going to a place of their choosing to review and copy the records. They might want to provide the records in a conference room of the court house or City Hall where they can keep an eye on you and the records. Be prepared to go there. Be sure to go there as soon as the records

are made available. The same or next day is preferable. Don't make them wait on you.

- When you review the records they provide, if you find that they have not provided everything requested, take note of it and ask the person who is working with you to please provide those records. Don't just drop it. Ask again and again until you get what you need.

What to request

To get to the heart of how a shelter is run, you need facts and figures, and then to analyze them in comparison with the other records. Here are some records you might want to request and analyze:

- Shelter intake and disposition records for the last three years.
- Shelter signed adoption and rescue agreements for the last three years.
- Shelter budgets for current year and the previous two or three years.
- Invoices related to shelter expenses for the last three years including but not limited to veterinary expenses, food, cleaning and sanitation supplies, medications, equipment purchases, building maintenance and improvement, and staff education and training.
- Personnel records for shelter staff members to see what training they have, and if they have had any disciplinary actions.
- Job descriptions for staff.
- Contract with the shelter vet who does the euthanizations, spay and neuters, and medical care.
- City and county ordinances that govern the shelter.

- Shelter forms, policies, and procedures.
- Receipt books for the last three years (if the shelter gives hand-written receipts) for rescues, adoptions, and returns-to-owners.

If there is something else you need, add it to your request.

Deliver the FOIA request

A FOIA request must be delivered to each person listed in your request. Your FOIA should be directed to every person who has input into the shelter policies and management. Here's a list of the usual suspects. Your list may change according to who is in charge locally.

- Mayor
- City Manager
- County Mayor or Manager
- Police Chief
- Every County Executive and Commissioner
- Every City Council member
- City and or County Attorney
- City and or County Risk Manager
- Members of an Animal Control Board or Committee

Complete your FOIA request, make an individual copy for every person shown on it, place the FOIAs in separate envelopes with the individual's name written on it, and deliver them to the County Office and/or City Hall. Ask the receptionist to ensure that they are given to the addressees as soon as possible, because they are time sensitive.

Post the FOIA on your social media and that you presented them to officials today.

What then?

According to Digital Media Law, government entities must respond to FOIA requests within twenty days. See: http://www.dmlp.org/legal-guide/time-periods-under-foia A response is either an acceptance or denial, not the provision of the requested records. They may take a "reasonable" time to provide the requested records. Consider that timeline as you plan your reform actions, especially if you have more than one FOIA. Posting the progress on your social media might compel the government to move the process along if they see others are watching their efforts. After ten days, you might want to send them an email requesting to know when they anticipate they will fulfill your FOIA request. Then do it again every Monday until they act. Keep the email chains for reference.

When they provide you with the information you request, be prepared to glean everything you can from it as soon as possible.

First, be prepared for one **or more** of your people to physically go to a place the government designates where they will provide the records for your review. Take a couple of copies of your FOIA request to be able to show them if they dispute what you requested. Then use your FOIA request to compare what was provided versus what you requested. Note anything that is missing, bring it to their attention right then, and ask for them to provide the information while you are there. If they say they cannot do it immediately, ask for a date certain and let them know you will follow up then.

If they did not provide copies of the requested information, you will need to make your own copies, so bring your own printer, ink, and paper. You do the copying so you are sure you have copies of everything for future reference and to share with your followers, media, or legal counsel. Bring plenty of paper to write on, as well. Spiral ring notebooks are easy to manage. Bring several.

You are there to make sure that your request has been fully met and to walk out with copies of the records. You can analyze the records later.

When you are sure you have everything requested, or a firm commitment from the government official when you will receive missing documents, take your copies and begin analysis. You may want to post on your social media that you have the documents, if anything is missing, and that you are in the process of analyzing them.

Because this is a time-consuming process, you will want to immediately deliver a second FOIA request if you have additional needs.

See Appendix 1 for a sample FOIA Request.

Chapter 10
Government Public Meetings

Your government is an interactive body. Your City Council and County Commissioners have regular public meetings in which they usually offer the opportunity for citizen input. Additionally, many cities and counties have some form of an Animal Control Board that gives guidance to the other government bodies about Animal Control and the shelter.

Get on the agenda

Check the agenda, which is usually available to the public ahead of the meeting, and see if public comment or input is on the agenda. If it is, as a local citizen, you may call and ask that you be placed on the citizen comment agenda. They may ask what you intend to address, because they have the right to limit citizen input to relevant matters. You might want to be as general as possible, saying something like, "animal welfare." If they press, let them know that you would like to discuss the animal shelter.

Remember to leverage everything you do. Post on your social media that you are requesting to be heard at the meeting, and post a copy of the official agenda. Post that you will follow up with more information about when you will speak.

If you are denied the opportunity to speak, in a new post, state that you were denied the opportunity, the reason they gave for the denial, who you spoke with, and when. Post that you will try again at the next meeting.

Your government is not bound by law to allow you to speak, so if you are denied, don't go screaming that your rights have been violated. But, be sure to post on social media that you asked and you were denied. At the very least, it shows that you are trying to address the government body and that they refused to listen.

Be prepared

If you are approved to speak, ask how long you will have. You will be limited to the amount of time you may take, which is often two minutes or less, so your pitch will need to be concise. Write it down and time it so you make sure you get the most important points spoken before your time is up.

Usually when your time is up, the body moves to the next citizen or agenda item, but just in case, be prepared for questions from officials. They may ask out of sincere consideration of your information, or to challenge you in an effort to deter you and anyone else from speaking out.

Post on social media in advance that you will be speaking and request that supporters come to the meeting to show citizen involvement. You may want to have ribbons or badges that supporters in the audience wear.

If you have more than one person who is allowed to speak, get together and determine who covers what material in their allotted time.

Your first time speaking may open the door with a simple outline of animal control statistics. You could begin like this:

"I am _____ representing [your group]. We are an animal advocacy group here to voice our concerns about the XXX Animal Shelter. I have before me the official records from the shelter that show the kill percentage at the shelter is 60 percent, which means that 60 percent of the animals that come under the control and custody of the shelter are killed there.

"As a tax-paying citizen, I am appalled at the high kill percentage, which means that the shelter is using my tax dollars to kill many homeless animals and lost pets. According to the records, these animals were killed because of XXXXXX...."

That's a start. You go from there to explain why their reasons for killing are unacceptable and fixable, and that you and your group are there to **help** reduce the kill percentage. Be prepared to explain how you can help if asked.

Bring with you your Reform Plan that details the problems as you see them and, very importantly, how your group can help overcome those problems. Be sure to include the names, phone numbers, and emails of people in the group who can be resources for the government officials. Have a copy of the document for every official member and media if they are there. Hand the document out before you approach the podium so it doesn't take away from your allotted time.

Be sure to post the document on your social media and tell your supporters that you gave it to the government officials.

If a second and third person in your group is allowed to speak, have them follow up with something that builds on your opening. Be sure they have hard numbers to back up what they say and are ready to defend their position.

No matter how incensed you are, no matter how righteously indignant you are, no matter how vehemently you abhor the people who make the decisions about the shelter, you must remain professional and in control during your interactions in public.

The second you lose your cool or start name calling or accusing people of being heartless, you will lose all credibility. While this is a life-and-death issue for you and the animals, it is simply a business issue to them. Compassion and common decency are not part of the business decision-making process.

Try to make friends, not make or antagonize enemies.

Take group business cards with you to hand to supporters and government officials.

Document your efforts

Have someone who is not speaking, video the entire interaction including follow-up discussions during the meeting and afterward with government officials. Also have people taking photographs. These videos and photographs are excellent to post on social media to show your commitment to the cause. They also put the government officials on notice that they cannot hide.

Also have someone take notes or record your portion of the meeting, or both. Then you can post a transcript, the recording, or both on social media. That will show your supporters, and detractors, that you are professional and what opposition you are encountering, and by whom.

Democracy is a participation-style government. Make it work for you and the animals.

Chapter 11
Empower Your Supporters

The key to a revolution of any kind is people speaking out. Grassroots reform starts with locals taking charge. Change must generate from local people and be locally driven, and then gain steam to include the entire world. But the seed of change comes from local citizens demanding change. If your citizens don't want it badly enough, it simply won't happen. If you are not willing to work on it, even while your heart is breaking and even when it looks hopeless, it won't happen. If you depend on some magic to happen while you sit by and wring your hands and whine, then animals will continue to be abused and murdered.

The revolution can start with just a few strong, committed people leading the charge. As the revolution gains momentum, like-minded people will join. But even if they don't, you alone can make it happen. You MUST make it happen.

In general, government-run animal shelters or pounds, especially in small, rural areas are notoriously hellish. The people in charge claim they are that way for a number of predictable excuses:

- Lack of money.

- Lack of staffing.

- We've always done it this way.

- They are just animals.

- People have tried to change it before and failed.

- It's the citizens' fault for not spaying and neutering their pets.

- The community doesn't care.

- We've got bigger issues to deal with.

- This takes time.

While some of those excuses may be true, especially those centering around funding, it doesn't have to be that way forever. By reforming, even funding issues can be alleviated.

You just have to make shelter reform a priority for them. And you can do that the easy way, by educating them, or the hard way, by forcing change.

First, try it the easy way. Try to work within the system and in a collaborative manner to bring about change. Try to find someone in power who is compassionate to be your champion. That champion might be within the government structure or a citizen who carries a lot of clout locally.

Educate your champion about:
- local animal-related ordinances

- state animal-related laws

- the economics of no-kill versus murderous shelters

- the realities of why shelters kill

- the impact of spay and neuter on shelter intakes

- abuse , cruelty, and neglect

- long-term strategies

- breed-specific legislation (BSL)

- dog fighting

- No-Kill solution

- why having a professionally run, no kill shelter is good public relations and image-building for your community

Empower your champion with facts and figures about your local shelter and national statistics. Then give your champion workable solutions she or he can present to people who can make a difference.

One champion is good. One champion backed by determined, vocal local citizens is an army of compassion and is very difficult for government officials to ignore.

Just like you need to educate and empower your champion, you need to educate and empower your compassion warriors, as well. Gather this information and post it where it is always available to your supporters or anyone who might happen to be snooping around your Facebook page to see what you're up to.

Then armed with facts, your supporters need to make their voices and demands known to the people who can enact change: government officials.

Make it easy for your supporters to contact those officials. The easier you make it for them, the more likely people will act. Government officials, especially elected officials, pay attention to numbers. The more local citizens who directly contact them, the more they pay attention. If they see their job is on the line next election, they will want to keep their constituency happy.

Empower your supporters with a readily available contact database or list of their officials. This list will be used again and again by your foundation of supporters and newcomers to your revolution.

- Place the list on your website.

- Post it on your Facebook page.

- Have it ready to print out to distribute at events.

- Have it so it can easily be emailed.

Here are your go-to lists:
- City officials – Mayor, council members, attorney, city manager, police chief.

- County officials – Mayor/Supervisor, commissioners/Supervisors, attorney, sheriff.

- State officials – Governor, pertinent committee chairs, Representatives/Assembly Members, Senators.

- Media contacts.

Once your lists are in place, you can make a call to action to your supporters on your Facebook page, website, and through your email list, and they will have the contact information readily available for immediate, coordinated and substantial engagement.

Traditionally, at least on the state level, personal telephone calls to an official's office carry more weight than an email. They pay close attention to an influx of telephone calls from their constituents and note the particulars about each call. The rule of thumb is that they assume that for every call they receive, there are ten more like-minded constituents. If you do the math, that says that 100 phone calls to an official translates in their mind to 1,000 interested parties, and so forth.

Email is also effective, especially for making more in-depth commentary. In an email, your supporters can state their position as well as educate their official about the issue and explain why it is important for the community. Additionally, emails can be sent in an email blast to many people at once.

Give your supporters easy, quick ways to engage your local officials.

Chapter 12
Call in the Media

The media is an extremely powerful tool to bring pressure on a government that won't work with you to reform a hellhole shelter. Because of the nature of media, and except for a lawsuit, it's the last thing a government wants dropped on them, so media must be used sparingly and wisely.

Public image is very important to governments. Exposing their incompetence, indifference, unprofessionalism, or illegal behavior gets them to pay attention.

Media basics

Here are some things to know about media:

- If it bleeds, it leads. As horrible as it is, violence, injury, and death are top stories, even in the animal or rescue world. Let's hope it doesn't get that far, but if it does, or there is even an eminent potential for it, call the media immediately.

Story hooks:

- Shelter is full, and they are threatening a kill day.

- Recent killing at the shelter due to policies like killing for room, killing right before a holiday so they don't have to work, or a disease outbreak which should have been handled professionally to save animals.

- The animals being kept in extreme heat or cold, or in the wind or direct sun.

- Shelter statistics that show a high kill percentage.

- Uncertified person doing the killing.

- Kill numbers reflecting a breed bias such as against Pit Bulls.

- Cruelty or neglect by a shelter staffer or volunteer.

- Unusually high number of animals missing, or killed due to alleged "aggression" or "unadoptable."

  • Second in terms of media interest would be mismanagement of taxpayer money.

Story hooks:
- Audit or citizen review of budgets and records reveals missing money.

- Money designated for the shelter used for something else.

- Contracts going to businesses without being properly bid out (veterinarian, renovation, etc.), or being paid to someone who could have a conflict of interest such as a government official or family member.

- Failure of the shelter to attempt to find homes or rescues for adoptable animals, especially showing that adoption/rescue brings in money versus killing COSTS money.

- Failure to spay or neuter BEFORE release, showing how that only creates more strays and killing for the shelter in the future.

  • Media are interested in corruption, lawsuits, and violations of law.

Story hooks:
- Shelter is not following laws or statutes on money, animal welfare, or stray hold times.

- Filing a lawsuit against the shelter.

- Corruption or bad behavior by a shelter employee that in any way pertains to the shelter.

- Unlawful banning of citizens from coming into the shelter or taking photographs in violation of Section 1983.

- Unlawful suppression of a citizen's right to free speech including speaking out about the conditions at the shelter, shelter statistics, animal treatment, holding civil protests, speaking to the media, or posting factual, non-defamatory or non-libelous information about the shelter on social media.

  - There must be a real story. Constant griping and conflict is not a newsworthy story. Allegations that cannot be substantiated are not a story. Personal vendettas are not a story. Screaming that they don't care is not a story.

  - Media must have someone willing to be quoted by name, to speak on camera, and to articulate the issue concisely. The media is not interested in anonymous sources, because they can be sued for libel or defamation if they don't have someone else who is knowledgeable about the situation making the claims and assertions of wrongdoing. They also need someone involved to bring a story to life. Just reading reports and facts will not get their attention. Those are used for background.

  - They like props and settings that look good on camera either for television or print. So they like people marching, people holding signs, dogs on leashes or in kennels, kids, speeches, people holding a swath of documents and pointing to them while they tell what they say, and animals in cages or kennels.

- The story must be able to be told in about a minute and a half on television. They may take a lot more time interviewing and gathering information, but they will usually edit the package down to fit a very tight time slot. Make everything you say pop. They work in soundbites, not tomes.

Print media is more flexible, but you still need to be concise and give them some good facts and quotes.

- Media loves soundbites – short quotes from an on-camera source that quickly sums up the story or draws interest. Soundbites are something like: "The mayor told us he would kill all the dogs." Or, "There seems to be some money missing." Or, "That poor dog died when its owner was coming to get it." Or, "No one, including an animal control officer should be allowed to be cruel to an animal." Or, "They are killing healthy, adoptable dogs." You get the idea. Be prepared with several kernels of truthful soundbites.

- They like a good setting or background. A stand-up interview in front of the shelter is always good. Other choices are the courthouse or dog park.

- They like research. Give them copies of documents, reports, photos, video, or voice recordings that support your story.

How to contact media

If you have enough lead time, you might want to look at past stories about animals to see which reporter has covered them and how sympathetic their stories were. Then, check out their Facebook page and see if they have photos of their animals. If they do, they might be very sympathetic to your story.

If you can, try to pitch the story to a sympathetic reporter. Go on the media's website and try to find the reporter's direct email or phone number. If you find it, write a very brief synopsis of your story, let them know who they can contact for more information, and give the contact number. Then either call or email the information to them.

If you cannot find a specific reporter's direct contact information, most media have a website that has a link or form where citizens can pitch stories. Use your synopsis to pitch the story there.

Pitch the story to every area print and broadcast media outlet.

Keep a list of who you contacted. Add each reporter who gives you a positive response to a media contact list in case you need them again.

What to do if media wants to do a story

- Be on time.

- Look professional.

- Bring documents with you.

- Be prepared to be able to clearly and calmly articulate your story in a succinct way. Don't ramble. Be sure to include your soundbites as you speak to the media.

- Do not curse, call names, or accuse anyone of being heartless or cruel. Talk about facts, not personalities.

- There is no such thing as "off the record." Do NOT say anything to a reporter that that you are not willing to see in print or on television.

Then what?

Once you get media traction, be sure to keep a list of each story and make copies of each one for future use in your PR strategy. Post the link to each story on your Facebook page, website, and a link to it in a Tweet. Encourage your followers to share the story far and wide.

Be sure to also download and save the media to a DVD or thumb drive in case the media outlet deletes the story later. Television stations will often leave the text portion of a story on their website but delete the video.

Chapter 13
Leverage Email

Marketing professionals know that email blasts can be one of the most effective tools for keeping supporters informed and for creating an immediate call to action.

Make sure you have email addresses of your supporters. Ask on your Facebook page and website for their email address. Create a newsletter that people sign up for, agreeing to allow you to send them email updates. Explain that by opting-in, they will get the inside scoop on everything happening within your group. Gather emails at events.

Once you have your list, do not share it with anyone else. Also, be sure your supporters' emails are not shown in the address bar. People expect, and rightfully so, that their information will be kept confidential.

You might want to create several lists:

- Core group members.

- Supporters.

- Local business people.

- Government officials.

- Media.

Your email lists can be used for a number of things:

- Requesting your followers to call their local officials about the shelter. You can add a link to your contact info that should be parked somewhere on your Facebook page or website. If not, just add the contact list in the body of the email.

- Fundraising.

- News about upcoming events like protests, government meetings, or media coverage.

- Updates on activities such as the status of FOIA requests, fundraising goals, lawsuits, and interactions with government officials.

- Hands-on information about how to do something like create signs for a protest.

- Letting government officials know your position on the shelter.

- Letting media know about the shelter.

- Asking businesses for help in reforming the shelter.

- Recruiting volunteers for hands-on activities.

- Newsletters.

MailChimp is an online, free, easy email service that automates your email blasts. You can customize email campaigns with their templates by adding photos, links, and logos. It performs list hygiene with an easy unsubscribe button in every email.

You can leverage your email blasts by coordinating them with other activities like speaking at city council meetings or having a protest. For instance, if you have a protest planned, you would send emails to your supporters, local government officials, and the media all at once.

Chapter 14
Organize a Protest or Demonstration

Sometimes the only way to get your government officials' attention is by a protest or demonstration. These are also valuable for gaining media coverage to bring attention to your cause, which will then gain supporters and apply pressure to government officials.

Remember that the goal of protests and demonstrations is to gain support, not to look like anarchists, or unhinged, hysterical animal nuts. Stand your ground, make your information known, draw attention to your cause, and educate the public, but be sure to do nothing that will paint you and your supporters as hotheads or irrational. Always take the high road when it comes to conduct. Be the voice of reason.

Even though your local government officials and their proxies may try to discourage, dissuade, impede, or even intimidate you into not holding a protest or demonstration, rest assured that you have a constitutional right to peacefully protest and demonstrate.

You have a right to peacefully assemble on public property. You have a right under the First Amendment to express your opinion and to say truthful things that the government may not like as long as it is not defamatory. The government, no matter what they tell you or try to intimate, cannot legally control or ban the CONTENT of your truthful speech.

They can, however, control the expression of how to conduct your assembly and free speech. They do have the right to control the reasonable time, place, and manner. They may require permits, restrict animals, times of day, or other details. They may prohibit loudspeakers. They may require that no trash be left, or that no food or drink be allowed. These restrictions are usually based on some larger perceived public good, like not disturbing other citizens, or not creating traffic hazards or dangerous situations. Follow their rules, but carry on.

According to the American Civil Liberties Union, the Constitution provides for your peaceful assembly at traditional public forums such as public sidewalks and parks, as well as plazas in front of government buildings, as long as you are not blocking ingress or egress, or intimidating other citizens.

Private property is much more restrictive unless you or someone in your group owns the property and agrees to the protest or demonstration. This means you cannot utilize private property such as businesses or residences for your event unless you have prior permission. The sidewalk, however, is considered public property. Just be careful to not restrict or impede the business's customers coming or going.

Set a date and time

You will want to set a date that will draw the most citizens. Saturdays often draw the largest crowds and spectators since people are off work and out and about. As soon as you know the date and time, start letting your supporters know. Once you have your permits approved, let the media know via a press release.

Choose a location

Even though you may want to protest in front of the shelter, these are usually located away from the public. You are seeking visibility, so a public place such as the town square may be a better choice. You will want a place that has good traffic flow to make it easy for your participants, and to draw the attention of passers-by. Make sure your location allows space for your event to not interfere with traffic flow in the street, on the sidewalks, or the entrances to buildings. Your event cannot be disruptive to other citizens.

By law, you have a right to protest or demonstrate on public sidewalks, government plazas in front of government buildings, and public parks.

Obtain permits

Many cities or counties require that you complete an application and receive a permit to hold a protest or demonstration. This process may take several weeks. You must follow the law, so be sure to check on this as soon as possible, allowing time to approve your application and issue your permit.

Although the government may have rules or restrictions on issues like a march route, the use of amplified sound equipment, or no sticks for signage, they cannot deny a permit simply because they don't like what you are doing, or because your event is in their eyes controversial. They also cannot legally so restrict your event to the point that it significantly interferes with your right of free speech and expression.

Check for permits and restrictions if you intend to:

- Have a donation bucket or ask for donations. Some localities require that you be a non-profit entity to ask for donations.
- Intend to use loudspeakers or have live music.
- Offer food, drinks, or products for sale.

Expect some reluctance on their part to issue your permit. Go about the process simply assuming that everything will work out fine. Be civil and non-confrontational. If someone tries to dissuade you, explain that you know your rights, and that you intend to exercise them.

Non-permit activities

Other forms of free speech or expression may be legally conducted without a permit. Distributing flyers or leaflets by hand to passersby on public sidewalks is legal as long as you do not in any way detain or accost citizens. Do not force people to take a flyer. Do not lay your hands on anyone. Do not block anyone's path.

If you want to set up a table with flyers or have any other physical structure, you may need a permit.

Peaceful picketing follows the same rules. Do not be disruptive or place anyone in danger. You may be able to conduct an orderly picket line on public sidewalks or plazas without a permit as long as you allow pedestrians to easily pass by and go into and out of buildings.

But just to be sure, always check with your local ordinances BEFORE your activity.

Set ground rules

Every event must have participant ground rules. Make them clear to your people. The basic ground rule is to be professional and beyond reproach at all times.

Pets – People will want to bring their pets. That's usually a bad idea, because of the potential that an excited dog could bite someone or get into a fight with another dog. Such an incident would be the focus of the media instead of your cause. Another reason is that most government entities mandate that you leave the protest site clean and unharmed. If dogs are allowed, you would have to clean up every poop before leaving. Better to leave the pets at home and concentrate on saving the shelter pets.

Behavior – Everyone must be civil and above reproach at all times. You must be seen as respectful, sane, compassionate people. You must not get arrested or become confrontational with the police or government officials. Take the high road.

- Do not allow alcohol or drugs.
- No weapons.

- No vulgar signage, speech, or gestures.
- No defacing or vandalism of property.
- Do not engage hecklers. Simply ignore them.
- Be sure to not accidently spill over onto personal property.

Interacting with police – Sometimes even the most peaceful event can take an ugly turn, especially if the opposition plants instigators in the crowd or has put law enforcement on notice to be very stringent in controlling the event. Be prepared by emphasizing to your supporters to not engage in any kind of arguing or confrontation with the opposition. Depending upon the mindset of your local government, planted antagonists or law enforcement may be lurking in the crowd (in uniform or in plain clothes) just waiting for one of your supporters to do something that could even remotely be deemed assault or disorderly, and then arrest, Tase, or pepper spray them.

Have a supporter or two videoing the protest and to be on the lookout for any confrontations between supporters and opposition or law enforcement, and to immediately start videoing any incidents.

If there is an interaction with police, the person making the video must stay several feet away from the conflict so they do not interfere with the police action.

Anyone involved with a police interaction should speak up clearly and calmly so the video cameras can get a useful recording of the incident.

If confronted by police, be exceedingly civil. Keep your hands out of your pockets and in plain sight at all times. Police are the authority and they will be assumed to be in the right, so you must be as cooperative and non-confrontational as possible. Do not give them any reason to escalate an interaction. Be polite. Do not run. Do not argue. Do not call names. Do not be a smart ass and tell them that you pay their salary, or to go catch some "real" criminals – that really makes them angry. Do not obstruct the police in any way. Do not touch a police officer. Do not raise your voice.

Do what they say without hesitation or backtalk. If they say to step away from somewhere, do so. If they say to show your hands, do so. If they say to put your hands behind your back, do so. If they say to sit down on the curb or elsewhere, do so. If they say to get in the patrol car, do so.

If you are handcuffed, put in a patrol car, or detained, ask – don't be antagonistic, but ask – if you are being arrested.

Keep your hands out of your pockets and visible at all times. Do not reach into a purse, backpack, or anything else that could remotely be construed as reaching for a weapon. The same goes if you are in your vehicle. Keep your hands on top of the steering wheel at all times. Do not reach for anything without first asking the officer if it would be okay to do so.

If asked for identification, give it to the officer. Explain that your ID is in your pocket, or backpack, or purse BEFORE you reach for it, and wait for an acknowledgement.

If asked why you are there, calmly explain that you are participating in a civil protest that you are allowed to do under your First Amendment rights.

If you are asked to leave the area, politely ask the officer if you have broken any laws. If asked to leave, do so immediately and do not resist or be argumentative. Leave the protest area immediately. If you feel that your rights have been violated, you can take care of it later. Right at this moment, you just need to not give the police any reason whatsoever to escalate the situation.

If you are arrested, do not resist. Totally comply to avoid escalating the situation and getting yourself hurt. Ask why you are being arrested. You can argue the lack of basis for your arrest when your attorney shows up.

Get the word out

Obviously the more people who participate in or attend your event, the better. Numbers are meaningful for several reasons. One is that your local government officials will surely be monitoring what's going on and how many citizens are interested. If they see that only a handful of people attend a protest or demonstration, they will interpret that as an indication that citizens don't really care, and therefore, their jobs won't be in jeopardy at election time if they ignore your demands.

Another reason for making sure you have numbers is that it looks good in media. Although television and photographers will usually concentrate on a cluster of people, if they can take a wide shot and show a lot of protesters, they will. Then that shows the audience that the protest was well supported and is important to local citizens.

But, even if just half a dozen people show, that's fine, too. Be visible. Be articulate. Be passionate. Make every voice count.

Get the word out by:
- Facebook page
- Facebook event
- Series of Tweets (Tweet storm)
- Ask your supporters to share the event on their pages
- Press release to local and nearby newspapers, television, and radio
- Flyers posted around town on approved places, especially on public bulletin boards in libraries, recreation centers, pet stores, laundry mats, and feed stores.

Be sure to give important details about your event: date, time, location, rules, request for signs, and, the location of the nearest public restroom.

Prepare

Make sure that the people in charge of the event have name tags so participants and media can easily identify you. Have blank stick-on name tags ready for people and ask (not demand) them to wear them. People who are not really supporters may be there and may refuse to wear a name tag.

Have an email sign-up sheet so people who are interested in updates can give their name and email address. You can use that list for a newsletter or email blast.

Have all equipment such as sound systems (if allowed) ready to use by the time the event starts. If amplified sound is not allowed, get a megaphone.

Have your own photographers and videographers cover the event. Be sure to have someone record the speeches in case the government officials try to claim defamation. You can use the photos and video to follow up on your Facebook page to keep interest up. Be sure to have someone watching for and videotaping any interactions between your supporters and the police and government officials.

Have places for people to deposit litter and be sure to clean the protest area immaculately before leaving.

A protest is a spectacle. It is highly visual, so be prepared. You want it to show well in photography, on television, and from people passing by in vehicles.

Here are some tips:

Visual

- Have a certain color that all supporters wear. Black is good, but it's hot. Red is always good.
- Have core group members wear identification badges so media can easily determine who is part of the group.
- Banners across tables that hold literature should be very colorful.

- Media is especially drawn to children, so make sure they have a sign and they know why they are there in case media asks them.
- Posters
- Collage of photos of the animals that have been killed.
- Collage of photos of animals neglected or abused.
- Group name.
- No-Kill information.
- Signs for protestors to carry and to place around the area.
  - Stop cruel heart stick
  - Stop cruel gassing
  - Compassion, not murder
  - Shameful
  - Disgraceful
  - Stop the slaughter
  - No excuse for animal abuse
  - Being cruel is not cool
  - No compassion, no peace
  - Killing is not the answer
  - Man's best friend – betrayed
  - Stop the killing
  - XX must go
  - Stop killing man's best friend
  - Stop the killing

- They deserve better

- Don't be sorry, do something – The Animals

- They trusted you

- Shelter of death

- Don't murder with my tax dollars

- Give us the truth and stop the abuse

- You have the power to stop animal abuse and murder

- Shame on XXXX Animal Control

- It's not euthanasia. It's murder

- You work for US!

- No-Kill NOW

- Where did the money go?

- Animals suffer here

- Taxpayers for accessibility and accountability

- We are watching you

- Cruelty is not the answer

- Compassion not corruption

- Lies

- Not a shelter – a killing field

- Honk for reform

- You stopped a beating heart

- Your lost pet could be killed at XXX

- Enforce animal welfare laws

- XXX Shelter – abusing animals in your community

- XXX Shelter murdering animals with your tax dollars

- Volunteers have a RIGHT to be in the shelter

- Animal abuse is a felony even for shelter staff

- Fire (shelter director)

- Animal control belongs to taxpayers

- Cruelty, neglect and murder must stop

- Too lazy to care

- Too greedy to care

- Volunteers banned

- If you have nothing to hide, let us in!

- No heat. No air conditioning. No compassion.

- What are my tax dollars paying for?

- Call your lawyer – you cannot ban me.

- 90% murder rate

- Puppy killers

- Kitty killers

- Tax payers for reform

- Voters for reform

Speeches

Someone needs to make a speech to the audience about why you are there, what you want to accomplish, and why it's important. The media will probably cover this. Have visuals like banners or posters behind the place where the speaker will stand so they will be seen in photography and on television.

Be sure to include statistics in the speech, as well as any incidences and conditions that exemplify why you are demanding reform.

If you can get a celebrity to make the speech, the media will be more likely to cover your event.

Education

If space permits, have a table or booth with educational materials to hand out such as shelter statistics, list of needed reforms, contact information for local and state government officials, animal abuse and neglect laws, photos of murdered animals, etc.

Opposition

It is not unusual for government officials or their informal proxies to try to covertly interfere with the event or to intimidate you and your supporters into not holding it. They will most likely have someone in the crowd.

One city even went to the length of quickly scheduling a Saturday morning re-paving project at the site of the protest the morning of the protest. They figured that people wouldn't walk a block to get to the protest. They were wrong, plus it gave us fodder to tell media, showing how sneaky and underhanded the government officials were. They did block the traffic that would have gone by, but that showed up in the media, as well.

Another opposition tactic is to have a mole spread the word that "undercover police" will be at the protest, taking photographs, and taking names and license plate numbers, so if you're there, you will be targeted by law enforcement later. That's a toothless threat if you are not breaking any laws. Stay legal and they can take all the names they want. It probably won't result in any problems for you.

General tips for protesters
- Keep your cool.
- Do not offer your personal information or information about the group's members or business to anyone other than a confirmed law enforcement official (and then only when asked).
- Have a plan to meet-up if you get separated from your group.
- Do not depend on having your cellphones. Write important information like phone numbers on your forearm in Sharpie. It will wash off, eventually.
- Stay hydrated. Bring water or Gatorade.
- Never pass up an opportunity to use a toilet.
- Wear comfortable shoes and weather-appropriate clothing.
- Don't carry anything you can't afford to lose.

DISCLAIMER

We are not attorneys and do not intend to provide legal advice. If you have questions, consult your attorney <u>before</u> undertaking any civil disobedience action.

Chapter 15
Facebook and Twitter

Facebook and Twitter are very powerful tools to expose animal control wrongdoing and inadequacies, and to help galvanize reform. An active and informative Facebook page and active Twitter account can disseminate information about shelter conditions, educate and empower your supporters, keep the world updated on your progress, and show government officials that you are serious about reform and that you have citizens behind you.

Create a Community or Business Facebook page specially designed to spread information, create interest, gain support, and to bring about pressure on government officials who can make changes. Make sure that it is a community or business page so you can gather statistical information (Insights) from it.

Keep in mind that this page will be seen by your supporters, by lurking government officials who want to find out what you are doing and want to shut you down, the media, and by people who will watch to see what you are doing and how you are doing it so they can start reforming their shelter.

Name this page something like: Reform XXXX [name of shelter] in [name of city] so there is no mistaking what the page is about. This makes the page easily found by supporters, government officials, and media.

Designate several people as Administrators so they can all post to the page and keep up with comments and notifications. It must be current and fresh every day. Every day.

Specifically request all of your current supporters and like-minded people to LIKE and share the page. Then ask them to specifically invite their friends to LIKE the page. You need to build a following. Also let your supporters know that if they click Get Notifications, they will be sure to get all of your posts. The more people who are behind you, the better, so do this weekly.

Clearly state your mission to bring about reform on your About page. Be professional. Be factual. No accusations or threats.

Post early and often

Keep the page active and fresh. Post at least daily, preferably several times a day. Keep people engaged and interested. Answer questions and respond to comments. If someone is a hater, simply delete them or ban them from the page. Do not engage the trolls. You are not there to argue. You own the page and you are allowed to control its content.

Information to post:

- Updates on contacts with government officials
- Updates on progress
- Government committee meetings
- Updates on the results of meetings
- Responses from officials
- Updates on Insights showing growing support. Post that the page has gained XX supporters, had XX people share information, had XX interactions, etc. This shows government officials and your supporters that your reform movement is being seen by a LOT of people, is growing, and is gaining momentum. Remind them that they never know who might be seeing this info: voters, potential businesses wanting to relocate, media, etc.
- Breaking news about other shelters that have been sued or that have chosen to reform
- No-Kill information
- Media links
- New Notes
- Photographs
- Videos
- Government official contact lists
- Pertinent ordinances or laws

- Calls to action
- Links to petitions
- Your Reform Plan of what needs to be done at the shelter and why
- Events such as protests, petitions, and meetings
- Requests for supporters to share the page
- Teasers about what is going on behind the scenes. For instance, if you or a supporter has filed a Freedom of Information Act (FOIA) request, just note it and tell your supporters that you will keep them updated on the progress and findings. That places the government officials in the spotlight and will compel them to abide by the FOIA rules.
- Or if you have met with an attorney, post that you have met and why and that you are making progress and that you will keep people updated. Don't divulge details such as the attorney's name or your plan of action. But posting about it will get government officials' attention.

Create Notes

These will be important to provide detailed information to your supporters. They are easily printed, downloaded, or shared.

Possible Notes:

- Government officials contact information. Never post private telephone numbers or addresses.
- Sample talking points to be used with media or when contacting government officials.
- Links to government meeting calendars and agendas, or just listings of the meetings.
- Your Reform Plan.
- Shelter statistics.
- Dates, times, and details about events.
- Links to media stories.

- Link and contact information about media contacts.
- Link to your petitions.
- Information about your protest including dates and times, rules, what to bring and not bring, and sign suggestions.
- Links to news items that are similar to your situation.
- Links to No-Kill organizations and Facebook pages.
- Copies of documents.
- Freedom of Information Act request template.
- Copies of responses to Freedom of Information Act (FOIA) requests.
- Progress notes on the status of activities like FOIA Requests.
- Copies of ordinances and laws, and links to them.

Create event pages

There is an event app you can use to set up and disseminate information about upcoming events such as:
- Protests
- Government meetings
- Group meetings

Create labeled photo albums

You may photograph the shelter and the animals in it as a concerned citizen and in an effort to ensure the animals are well cared for and to help find them homes. Photography at a tax-payer-funded facility that is not a national security risk such as a government-run shelter is an expression of the First Amendment right of Free Speech, according to the American Civil Liberties Union (ACLU). Allowing such photography is a part of the peoples' right to hold our government accountable.

Here's a link to a story about how the ACLU stepped in and educated an animal shelter about how they violated citizens' rights by banning photography. http://www.aclu-md.org/press_room/189 http://www.baltimoresun.com/news/maryland/baltimore-county/north-county/bs-md-co-aclu-animal-shelter-20141016-story.html

But you must obtain all photos legally. It is legal to photograph all things that are plainly visible from public spaces including government buildings and government officials in the performance of their official duties. Do not trespass on private property to obtain photographs.

It is legal to have a long lens and to photograph the shelter from another public place if the shelter does not allow photography. Don't photograph people in private places like their homes or vehicles. Do not photograph people in private situations. You are only interested in their official behavior. Never photograph children or minors for any reason. Do not follow around or stalk anyone for any reason.

Here is an excellent link about your photography and videotape rights: https://www.aclu.org/know-your-rights/photographers

Photograph (so you own the photos) and post on your Facebook page:

- the shelter's facilities and conditions
- the condition of animals in the shelter
- the sanitary conditions or lack thereof in the shelter
- your events
- your protests
- media interviewing people about your story
- animals' conditions as they are released from the shelter
- Animal Control Officers in public places including loading and unloading animals

Videotaping

While it is legal to photograph people in public places without their permission, it is NOT legal to videotape them in such situations, because the audio portion of the video could constitute a wiretap violation.

Just as when making an audio recording, unless you are ***personally*** involved in the interaction with the person being videotaped, you cannot legally videotape them. Ask your attorney about this prior to videotaping anyone.

Videotaping government meetings such as city council meetings or county commissioner meetings and public forums is legal. If they try to stop you, make sure you have witnesses, ask them why, comply so you are not arrested, and then notify media. Write about it on your Facebook page giving specific details and asking why a government agency that runs on taxpayer dollars is so secretive.

Manage your page

You must aggressively, continuously manage your Facebook page. Don't let it go dead or you will lose momentum or not be taken seriously. Post something important every day. Every day!

Don't let haters or dissenters hijack the page or a post. Be sure that all posts are professional and civil. You must claim the high ground to be taken seriously and to keep from being sued for defamation. Immediately delete all name calling, hate speech, threats, slurs, incorrect information, inappropriate comments, graphic photos, sexual photos or information, photos of minors, and defamatory comments. Block people who are disruptive.

Encourage your supporters to SHARE your posts on their personal pages. Tell them HOW to share best (copy, paste). This increases exposure and puts more pressure on government officials.

Keep your Facebook reform page on point and focused. Do not dilute your message with extraneous information. No cutesy posts. No funnies. No sharing and cross-posting animals. Reform-directed information **only**.

Be sure to continually copy everything on your page and park it in a secure location (on your own computer) that is NOT a Facebook page in case the page somehow gets deleted. You can do this using Screenshots, Microsoft Snipping Tool, or the app Jing. This will come in handy to ensure that you have a history of what everyone says and does. It could also come in handy in case you are accused of defamation.

Twitter

As we know from political leaders, Twitter can be a powerful tool to create instant exposure and response. You need to create a Twitter account for your group. Try to include "Reform" and the name of your city or shelter in your Twitter handle. For instance, @ReformSmithville.

Make sure to ask all of your supporters to follow you on Twitter and to re-Tweet your Tweets to gain exposure. Post your Twitter handle on your Facebook About page.

Then get on Twitter and follow like-minded Tweeters. They will often follow you back. Be sure to follow the people and departments who are pertinent to your mission such as your supporters, politicians, government officials and departments, animal welfare organizations, etc. Leverage their Tweets by re-Tweeting them with no response, or re-Tweeting them with your response attached to it.

You can go to the settings of your Twitter page and allow it to automatically post everything you Tweet to your Facebook page, which is a timesaver and creates interest in it.

Then become a Twitter ninja. Look at other Tweets and see how the masters do it. You only have 140 characters and a photo to get your message across.

The most effective Tweets are targeted: they include appropriate hashtags, and when necessary, are directed to someone else's Twitter handle. People often get notifications or seek out Tweets to look at by the hashtag. Tweets to someone's Twitter handle go directly to their Notifications.

If you put "RT" at the end of your Tweet, it politely asks other people to re-Tweet your Tweet, which increases exposure.

Possible hashtags:
- #reform
- #animalwelfare
- #rescue
- #shelterreform
- #animals
- #protest
- #NoKill
- #KillList
- #cats
- #dogs

Make a list of people who you want to direct Tweets to so you can use them again and again. Consider:
- Governor
- Mayor/Supervisor
- Shelter
- Council members
- State Senators, Representatives, Assembly Members
- Your U.S. Senator and Representative
- Your shelter
- Rescues

Use eye-catching photos to make your point. If you have photos of the animals or even the shelter, use them. Make sure you have ownership of the photos to avoid copyright problems. Do not use anything graphically cruel or violent or you will get reported and possibly banned from Twitter for a couple of days.

Make your Tweets have impact. Call out people in charge. Don't call them names or threaten them, but ask them questions, or quote stats, or inform them of what needs changing.

For instance:@mayorsmith Have you even BEEN to the @Acme shelter? It's cruel & inhumane. Go take a look. Then change it! #Reform #ShelterReform RT

Or: @Acme you've killed 209 dogs for space so far this year. How can you justify this mass slaughter? Go #NoKill. @Mayor @governor #reform #animalcruelty RT

Or: @staterep do you understand how it looks for our state that @Acme kills 85% of their animals? The world is watching. They can do better. Go No-Kill. #reformshelter #state RT

Or: @mayor @CouncilMember could you personally murder the animals @Acme shelter murders every week? If not, how can you allow others to do it for you? Shameful. #reform RT

You can pin a Tweet to the top of your timeline at any time. Use this option often.

If you get an interesting response on a Tweet, take a screenshot or Microsoft Snip of it, save it, and post it to your Facebook page.

When someone follows you, always thank them with a Reply or a Direct Message on Twitter.

If someone blocks you and it's someone like a government official or politician, take a screenshot of the blocked message and then Tweet that out telling the world who they are and that they blocked you. Then post it to Facebook.

Your Twitter Profile page has a place to see your Tweet activity. That shows you how many people have seen your Tweets and interacted with it. Use these numbers (screenshot) to Tweet out to the decision makers showing them how many people are watching them and their responses. For instance: @mayor @shelter @governor This Tweet about the shelter's killing for space got 2,500 exposures so far. Disgraceful. The world is watching. #Reform now. RT

You can also use Twitter to get exposure for specific animals on kill lists or special needs, etc. Include a photo. Ask for a RT. Additionally, Tweet out events, press coverage, and anything that is happening with your mission. Do NOT dilute your Twitter feed with Tweets of cutesy photos or videos or memes. This is all business. If you clutter up your Twitter feed with non-reform or non-rescue Tweets, you'll lose followers. We all have too much to look at without having to wade through cuddly kittens while others are dying.

Just like your Facebook page, keep Twitter alive and active for greater results.

Chapter 16
Election Time

Many of the people who have the ability to change how your shelter is run are elected officials. The one thing elected officials care about the most: getting elected again.

You can use election time to determine their position on animal welfare, the shelter, and other animal-related topics. Then, you can lock them into those positions – if they are supportive to the animals – or educate them as to why they should be supportive.

By creating a survey or questionnaire for incumbents and first-time office seekers, you can determine which candidates will receive your endorsement. Caution: your state may prohibit not-for-profit entities from engaging in political activities such as endorsing candidates. If that is the case, you can still do the survey but NOT endorse any candidate. You simply publish their answers without evaluating them.

Check out the sample questionnaire in the Appendix. You are welcome to use it as you see fit. Pick and choose questions that are pertinent to your particular situation. Add others that may not be listed. Be sure to ask whatever addresses the problems at your shelter.

The timing is important for your survey. It must be in their hands a month BEFORE the election. You may contact candidates and ask them if they prefer to have a printed copy of the questionnaire or if you may send it to them via email.

Give them a week to complete and return it. Then you have a week to do analysis and to publish your results, giving your audience prior information of who is and is not animal-friendly.

Every step of the way, let your followers know about the survey. This puts candidates on notice that they are expected to participate. Here are some quick announcements to use about the survey you can use in your social media:

- Reform XXXX has created a Candidate Animal Welfare Issues Questionnaire for incumbent and first-time office seekers to determine their views on animal welfare issues. We will be giving the questionnaire to the candidates next week. We will keep you posted as to the process.

- Our Candidate Animal Welfare Issues Questionnaire is now in the hands of every candidate. The deadline for the return of the survey is XXXX. We will keep you posted as to our progress.
- The deadline for returning our Candidate Animal Welfare Issues Questionnaire was yesterday. We have received completed questionnaires from XXX, XXX, XXX, and XXX. We did not receive completed questionnaires from XXX, XXX, and XXX. We have begun analysis of all responses, and will share them with you as soon as we get them organized. Stay tuned.
- The results of our Candidate Animal Welfare Issues Questionnaire are in. Feel free to take this information to the voting booth with you.

When you publish your results, list each question, then each candidate's response. If a candidate did not answer or did not return the questionnaire, note that as well to show they chose to not answer.

For instance:

1. If elected, what improvements to the shelter's facility will you promise to work to make in a timely manner?

John Smith: I will try to have heating and cooling installed to ensure better environmental control for the animals.
Mary Jones: I will look into procuring more kennels for the animals.
Bill Marshall: Did not return the questionnaire.
James Johnson: Did not answer the question.
David Williams: I do not believe that I will be able to have an impact on the shelter facilities.

Once you have compiled your results, you may want to create a press release and send it to local media (newspapers, TV, radio) a week or more before the election.

Be sure to save all candidate responses and communications in a safe place in case a candidate disputes your analysis, and so you can remind them of their answers should they be elected.

Chapter 17
Petitions

Petitions are an excellent way to show that you have the support of the community behind your efforts to reform the shelter. They are easy to create and to use to apply pressure on government officials, and to gain supporters.

Petitions are directed to the people who can make change. You are "petitioning" them to hear your voice, your concerns, and to act on them. In this case, you will direct your petition to everyone who can do that, not to the shelter staff, who are simply doing a job. Whoever has official input and decision-making authority into how the shelter is run should be listed.

Be specific about what you want. Don't be vague and just say you want improvements. A coat of paint on a feces-smeared wall would be an improvement, but not real change. This would be where you would insert portions of your Reform Plan. Specifically state something along the lines of:

"We the undersigned demand that the Acme Animal Shelter immediately enact reforms that will improve the conditions for the animals at the shelter, and that they increase the live-release rate to 95% or above.

Necessary changes include but not limited to:

- Making the kennel areas of the shelter environmentally safe and humane for all animals in terms of temperature control.
- Creating sufficient kennel areas so that gang kennels are eliminated, with no more than two animals per kennel.
- Separation of male and female animals to prevent fights and pregnancies.
- Separation of young dogs from the general population to help prevent parvo infection.
- Adopting industry standard sanitation and infection control procedures and policies.
- Provision of basic vaccinations and healthcare medications for all incoming animals within 24 hours of intake.

- Allowing volunteers into the shelter to help find homes and rescues for the animals.

Create a petition

The easiest, most respected petition site is Change.org. They make the process easy to create and maintain a petition, and it has tools you need to analyze the results of your petition. Go there and follow directions. Prime the pump with several signers with comments. Then, get the word out about it. The more people who sign your petition, the better.

Publicity

When your petition is live, make a big splash on all your social media about it. Then follow up asking people to sign it and share it every few days. If you have an email list, share it that way. Keep asking people to sign and share. Don't let it go fallow or it will send the message to government officials that it was just a flash in the pan and that only those people care.

You could also have printed petitions and send supporters out who can articulate what the petition is about to gather signatures around town. Follow all laws about where you can do this. Public property is usually fine as long as you don't interfere with people's ability to come and go and you don't accost people. A sign asking for signatures to support shelter reform may help draw attention to your cause.

Save the printed signatures so you can produce them along with a printout of the online signatures.

Analysis

Once you start gaining signatures, you can begin analysis and then share your analysis on your social media (Facebook) to put pressure on government officials. Give petition updates often, especially at first when you see the initial surge of signatures. As time goes on, you'll have more data to share. Keep up the pressure. Here are some ideas:

- PETITION UPDATE! We had 50 more people sign our petition within the last 24 hours! Momentum is growing! People are behind us.

- PETITION UPDATE! We have 1,000 signatures for our petition that demands that government officials reform the animal shelter. I bet they could use those 1,000 voters when re-election comes up.
- PETITION UPDATE! Of the signatures, XX% are local citizens. These are taxpayers and voters! These people are holding local government officials accountable for how our tax dollars are used and they demand that the shelter be reformed.
- PETITION UPDATE! We're on a roll! People all across the United States are signing our petition. Too bad the exposure for the city is for such a cruel act. This isn't good for economic development! What company would want to come here knowing that the government is cruel to homeless animals and lost pets, and unresponsive to citizens' demands for reform!
- PETITION UPDATE! Look at what Jane Doe from XXXX says: "XXXXXXXXXXX." She hit the nail on the head!
- PETITION UPDATE! We see that many people from all across the country are viewing our petition. Could be media. Could be businesses. Could be law enforcement. Who knows?

Now what?

Your online petition tool allows for you to be able to print out the petition and signatures. You also may have the paper signatures you collected. The next step, after you feel you have a significant number of signatures is to present the printed petition to the people in government at a public meeting. Have your supporters show up and take photos and video.

Ask to be on the agenda to discuss the need for reform of the shelter. When it is your time to speak, concisely explain the petition and that you are officially presenting it to the parties who have the ability to make the changes. Say something along the lines:

"Members, I have here a petition demanding reform of the XXX Shelter. It has XXXX signatures from local voters and citizens all over the United States who are appalled at the conditions of the shelter and demand that the shelter be reformed to become a place of real shelter, not of cruelty and death. I present this to you on behalf of the XXXX animals who have been killed by the shelter in the last year."

Then walk up and lay the petition in front of the head honcho. "I'd be happy to answer any questions any one may have about our demands."

They probably won't ask, but just in case you have a compassionate member, be sure to be able to answer any questions in a professional, calm manner. Have solutions to their usual objections like lack of budget or that they are "looking into it."

Petitions are just one more tool to apply pressure on government to do the right thing. And, as with other strategies, you must work it for it to be effective.

Chapter 18
Public Relations

Public relations is how you mold your image and reputation, and create loyalty. Rest assured that your detractors will be out there trying everything in their power to discredit you and your efforts. To counteract that damage, you must have an active public relations strategy.

What PR is not
- Name calling
- Threatening
- Smearing
- Lying
- Hyperbolic (over the top) language

What PR is

- Creating a positive image of your organization and goals
- Building a positive reputation for your organization
- Creating trust in your organization
- Educating people about your organization and goals
- Creating loyalty to your organization

Daily PR
Everything you do in relation to your organization on a daily basis either helps or hurts your public image. You are either getting better or getting worse. Playing nice until you meet with a challenge and then blowing up and acting like a jerk, flips all your hard work back to ground zero or even worse.

It's more difficult to bring someone back into the fold after a PR disaster than it is to continue to reinforce and cultivate a supporter every day.

You have PR opportunities every day. For instance, when you see someone with their dog, strike up a conversation. Tell them that you, too, love dogs and that you are a member of Reform XXXX, working toward helping reform the shelter. Don't be hateful and scream about the shelter or the government officials. Take the opportunity to educate that person about your plans and goals. Give them a business card and let them know you'd love to have their help.

Take advantage of everyday PR opportunities.

PR portfolio

If possible, enlist the help of a professional writer or PR person to help you. If you can't, find a supporter who writes professionally to help. You will be judged by your professionalism. Poor grammar, spelling, punctuation, and sloppy writing gives people the impression that you are not a serious, professionally run organization.

Create a portfolio of PR pieces that you can use at a moment's notice to educate and sway someone.

Here's a list of PR pieces for your portfolio:

- A logo you will use on everything.
- Business cards.
- Brochure explaining what your organization is, your goals, and contact information.
- Fact sheet showing the kill rate at your shelter versus a no-kill shelter.
- Fact sheet showing the steps toward making a shelter no-kill.
- Newsletters.
- Printouts of blogs written by or about your organization.
- Fact sheets with information from reputable organizations showing various issues like need for spay/neuter programs, minimum sheltering requirement for animals, animal welfare laws and ordinances, and refuting breed-specific ordinances,
- Copies of positive PR about your organization in the media.

- Printout of a collage of activities such as protests and speaking at government meetings.
- Copies of Section 1983.

Create PR opportunities

Sometimes you have to create PR opportunities. You can offer information and education as the primary focus of your engagement, and then gently bring in the goal of reforming the shelter (without bashing the shelter). Here are some ideas:

- Speak to civic groups about the importance of spay/neuter.
- Participate in community festivals and events.
- Speak to church groups.
- Present educational programs to school classes.
- Create a press release on how to locate your lost pet. At the end, note that Reform XXX is a group of citizens working toward reforming the shelter and taking it to no-kill status, and give your contact information.
- Create 15-second public service announcements (PSAs) for local radio stations to read about spay/neuter, micro-chipping, etc. Then tag at the end with, "A public service announcement by Reform XXX."

Other PR tools

- Blog – Create a blog and have supporters write about what your organization is doing and the importance.
- Press releases – Create and send press releases to the media about your organization's activities.

- Email blitzes notifying supporters of current issues, fundraising, and activities.
- Someone to create memes – Photos draw more attention to Facebook and Twitter posts. Use only photographs and art that you have a right to use.
- Public meetings where you explain what you are doing and ask for volunteers. Public libraries often allow citizens to hold meetings there for free.

Some helpful, free programs are:
- Fotor is a quick, easy, free program to add text to photos and to create memes.
- Jing allows you to take much bigger screenshots than Microsoft Snippet.
- MailChimp is a free email blitz program.
- If you use your own printer, you can get good-quality ink less expensively from Castle Ink.

Chapter 19
Rescues are Crucial

While you're busy trying to reform the shelter, animals languish there or worse. One of the very first steps in reform should be to get the shelter to allow you to start saving more animals. Rescues are part of that strategy.

Rescues are crucial for successful no-kill shelters, as adoptions alone will not cover the sheer numbers of dogs and cats that come into shelters, especially during puppy and kitten seasons.

Establishing strong connections with reputable, dependable rescues is an essential component of achieving and maintaining an enduring no-kill status. It requires research, diligence, and good communication to establish and support good rescue partnerships – it is hard work, but animals' lives are at stake. Following this chapter's guidelines will enable you to make these connections and develop strong, reliable partnerships.

Your first step in making rescue contacts is determining who (whether an individual or several people) in your group is willing to invest the time to research rescues, make contacts, and follow through. You **must** do the research. There are thousands upon thousands of rescues in this country, but many are not true rescues and must be avoided.

Fighters, bunchers (individuals who sell animals to laboratories), abusers, and hoarders often set up a fake rescue to more easily obtain their victims. There are rescues that overload themselves, fail to properly vet the animals in their care, fail to screen potential adopters, fail to keep the facilities clean and the animals are living in filth, and so on.

Social media, and especially Facebook, is an excellent source of rescue listings and their activities. Use the internet – Google your state+dog/cat/animal rescue and you'll get a list. Search other shelters' Facebook pages for their posts of rescues.

Make sure to include different types of rescues in your list. Many are breed-specific, or just accept elderly animals, young animals, or small animals. You should find rescues for every contingency you may encounter.

Once you target appropriate rescues, you must investigate them before placing animals with them.

If you are considering a rescue outside your immediate area, your first contact should be their local animal control. Ask them if they have had any problems or complaints about the rescue, and if they consider them to be reputable.

The rescue community in a region is often tight. Rescues usually know each other or know about each other. Ask fellow rescuers about rescues you are considering.

Questions

The next step is to ask the potential rescue about their operation.

- What are their adoption policies?
- Do they spay/neuter and completely vet their animals before adoption?
- Do they require home visits?
- Do they require vet references and personal references?
- Do they check out addresses of potential adopters?
- Do they house animals in their facility or do they use fosters?
- How do they assess potential fosters?
- Do they have an adoption agreement (very important) and explain that you require a copy of it before working together.
- Ask for the names and addresses of their veterinarians.

Questions for a rescue's veterinarian:
- How long have you known this rescue?
- Would you consider this rescue an average, excellent, or poor rescue?
- Does the rescue have their animals spayed/neutered before adopting them out?
- Does the rescue ensure that their animals are up to date on all vaccinations and heartworm preventive?
- Have you ever seen any signs of animal abuse, injury, or neglect for which you felt the rescue was responsible?
- Do you feel that the rescue is able to manage their animals well or are they overloaded?
- Do you feel the rescue is financially sound?

You must make sure you are contacting the right rescues to pull from your shelter. You might even consider going on Google maps to view the addresses the rescue provides. Street level and overhead views can show you the conditions in and around the rescue and if there appears to be squalor, signs of dog fighting, or overcrowding.

Jump into action

Once you have a rescue that has checked out and is willing to pull animals from your shelter, make sure you have their correct contact information – email as well as phone numbers. Many times you will only have hours to save a dog or cat, and you must be able to reach the rescue contact as quickly as possible.

Keep in mind that rescues are bombarded daily with requests from scores of shelters and pounds, and they cannot take every animal needing to be saved. A shelter group that is quick to act, can provide detailed information on each animal, and can help arrange fee payments and/or transport to the rescue will often be considered ahead of other requests.

Do not expect the rescue to pull animals every time you ask, so building a list of solid rescue contacts will help you save more animals from your shelter. If the shelter will agree, offer minimal or zero fees to the rescues. If that is not possible (most shelters are tied to local government, and some cannot adjust their fees), then post on Facebook that you need a specific amount of donations for pull fees for each animal that rescues have committed to. If you have an email list of supporters, send a quick email to them, as well. There are many people who love animals and cannot do shelter/rescue work, but are willing to donate to help make it happen. Don't be afraid to beg!

You will need to set up an easy, secure way for people to donate well ahead of time. PayPal is one of those mechanisms, but it charges a small fee. Be sure to include the cost of those fees in your donations plea.

Make the pitch

When contacting rescues, make sure you provide ALL details about the animal or animals you are asking them to consider. DO NOT hide facts or lie. Doing so will forever alienate that rescue. Remember, too, rescues talk to other rescues. Honesty and reliability are critical.

Here is what you need to be able to provide to them:

- approximate age
- approximate size and weight
- breed or breed mix (to the best of your knowledge – often it's hard to be exact)
- any medical issues (however minor) including heartworm status
- any vetting that has been done – spay/neuter, dental, vaccinations
- temperament
- good photographs (hopefully of a happy, fun animal)

- their history – were they an owner surrender, hoarding case, stray, owner moved, owner died, etc.
- urgency – are they about to be killed in the shelter (be honest)

Temperament

Again, do not hide anything! Temperament is a major issue for rescues. They will need to know:
- if the animal gets along with other animals
- un-safe for children for any reason
- food aggression or resource guarding
- fear biting
- fearful of men/women/adults/children
- can be handled or touched
- housetrained
- crate trained
- barker
- escape artist
- knowledge of basic commands
- leash trained
- energy level (laid back, couch potato, rambunctious, great hiking partner, etc.)
- any known fears or behaviors that may need addressing

Your honesty about every animal will pay off. In the past, we have had dogs with temperament issues accepted by our rescue partners because we had always been up front and honest about each and every dog we asked them to consider. Rescues also understand that an animal who exhibits aggressive behaviors may be showing signs of fear or stress due to the kennel setting or strange circumstances. These behaviors often disappear once the animal is in a secure, calm situation.

Solid commitment

It is an absolute must that everything is solidly in place BEFORE you pull the animal from the shelter. You must establish your reliability and expertise with both the shelter and the rescue in order for your ultimate goal of no-kill to be achieved. Sloppy handling of details will alienate both parties, and all your efforts can backslide very, very quickly.

When pulling an animal from the shelter for a rescue, make sure the following details have all been put in place:

- The shelter has all the information they need for their records about the rescue.
- Any pull fees and/or vetting fees are covered prior to the animal leaving the shelter.
- The rescue has all the information about the dog or cat that they need (health, temperament, special needs, etc.).
- A person is in place to "pull" the animal at a set time from the shelter, unless the rescue has a volunteer coming to pull.
- If the animal is not going directly to the rescue, a temporary foster or pre-paid boarding must be in place to hold the dog or cat until time to go to the rescue.
- If any vetting is to be done prior to the rescue taking possession, this must be scheduled before pulling the animal and plans MUST be in place for transport to and from the vet.
- Transport to the rescue MUST be in place prior to pulling the animal.

A smooth transition from the shelter to the rescue is not only the best for the animal, it also helps ensure future pulls by that rescue. Establishing your credibility as knowledgeable and reliable not only solidifies your relationship with that rescue, it also establishes your reputation throughout the rescue community.

Transporting

Transporting animals to rescues can be quite the challenge at times. Volunteers who will donate their time and vehicle to help transport are "gold"! If a rescue is several hours away, posting the need and details on Facebook can often get volunteers to drive portions or "legs" of the trip.

Another possibility is to use one of the many transport groups that have pages on Facebook. Each has their own procedures they use and that must be followed. Just make sure whoever is helping with transport is reliable. One person not doing their part will end up with a driver and an animal sitting somewhere with no plans in place! That is dangerous for the transporter and the animal.

By establishing solid rescue relationships, which is always an ongoing process and should never stop, you will be able to save more animals than by relying on just adoptions. Be thorough in your research, accurate in your animal descriptions, reliable in your process, and you will see more and more animals saved from your shelter and able to live happy, well-loved lives. It takes hard work by dedicated people, and it is worth every minute spent when you see a dog or cat leave the shelter and know that it is safe.

Adoptions

Just to be clear, we are not saying adoptions aren't important! Adoptions are the backbone of saving shelter animals, so they should be a top priority, as well.

You can help the shelter reach more potential adopters by networking the animals through social media and adoption sites like PetFinder. If the shelter doesn't already have a Facebook page, start one! Post photographs and information on each animal, and always include the location and phone number of the shelter. Keep these postings up to date, and you will reach more adopters. Creating and maintaining an active, responsive, helpful Facebook page will greatly increase exposure for every animal in your shelter. Be prepared to answer questions and to help coordinate adoptions.

Shelter requirements for adopters vary widely. Tragically, many have little or no requirements and will adopt to anyone who pays the fee, placing the shelter animal at risk of being taken for breeding, fighting, bait, flipping (getting a homeless dog or cat and selling it), and being sold to labs for research. If this is the case with your shelter, this must be addressed in your Reform Plan.

Ensuring your shelter spays or neuters the animal BEFORE releasing it to an adopter or rescue absolutely guarantees that the animal will not be used by a breeder and will not produce any more litters. If your shelter does not do this, address it in your Reform Plan.

Fees and what they cover have a wide variation also. Work with your shelter on improving their adoption requirements and thereby helping to ensure a good, loving home for each animal.

Helping the shelter to increase adoptions to citizens, as well as your continued rescue work, will both have a significant impact on the numbers of animals in the shelter and result in lowering the kill percentage.

Finally, keep in mind that even government entities like to be seen as successful. They may not give one hoot about the animals, but they like to be seen as doing a good job. Your success in helping them increase their live-release rate makes them look good and saves taxpayers money. It doesn't really matter who gets the credit, as long as the animals are saved. If their ego needs stroking by letting them look like heroes, fine. Maybe that will compel them to work with you on other issues.

As we always say, "It's about the animals."

See the Appendix for sample rescue adoption forms.

Chapter 20
Overcoming Your Fears

Now you've studied the guidelines, you know your mission, you WANT to make this change happen, but you've hit a wall. Something is holding you back, right? You're now a little hesitant to become the center of controversy. Well, that's very understandable – we are human, and we have fears. BUT, the animals NEED you to overcome that fear, that hesitancy. Their lives depend on you, and that alone will give you strength!

Here's a list of common fears, and what you need to do to overcome them:

- **I've never done anything like this before.** We've all felt that! Reforming an animal shelter is not your every day, normal task! Don't let feelings of inadequacy, inexperience, or fear of failure stop you. Your passion for the animals is what will drive you and keep you going. It's a learning process, and that is why we wrote this book, to help you along the way.

- **I can't look at the animals, knowing they might die.** This is exactly why you are on this mission! If you are at the point of fighting for change, then you've already been fighting to save the animals on a regular basis. You need to see their faces, their eyes, and feel their fear, their longing for love. Look at them for inspiration, for courage, for determination to fight the fight and not stop.

- **It's a small town/the government officials will retaliate**. It doesn't matter about the size of the town, or city, or community. People will take sides on this, without a doubt. Yes, people will mock you, will argue, will point fingers, and will dismiss your mission by saying, "they're just animals." But for every person who is against you and what you want to accomplish, there's a person who is supporting you, believing in your mission, and may at some point step forward to help you.

Government officials will demean you, and they will argue against you, and they will publicly state you are full of it; but they won't retaliate per se. They can't legally. You have the facts, you have the stats, and you can answer back for every negative statement they make. Eventually they will either join your mission and work with you, or they will step out of it. Public outcry is key to forcing local officials to make positive changes.

- **They will call me the crazy dog lady.** So what? We think that's an honorable description! Being called the crazy dog lady, or cat lady, or animal nut, is a compliment in our book. It just affirms your passion and your mission, so wear it proudly and keep on track!

Do not let the naysayers and social media trolls affect you. There are people who live to attack others, and it's their problem, not yours. You have to develop a thick skin – your mission is on target, and you don't have time to fool with idiots. Ignore them and focus on your purpose! When you finally achieve your goal, and your shelter is now no-kill, you won't hear all these small-minded individuals, for you have shut them up.

Be strong, be determined, and keep always in your mind, "I'm saving the animals." That is ALL that matters!

Appendix 1
Sample FOIA Request

This is a sample FOIA Request Template for you to edit according to your situation. What language your state requires may vary somewhat, but this is a start.

[Date]
Freedom of Information Act
[Tennessee] Open Records Act
Request

[Your name
Your address]

Referred to:
[Name of official and title]
[Name of official and title]
[Name of official and title]
Include as many officials as possible]

Dear Administrators:

Pursuant to Freedom of Information Act, and the [Tennessee] Open records Act, I am requesting to view or to be provided copies of the following public records:

1.   The intake forms and disposition information on the following dogs with the ID numbers shown below. The documents on each dog should include each Intake Form, and the receipt for payment to the XXXX Shelter, OR the Intake Form and an invoice from [shelter vet clinic] showing the dog by ID number and the date of euthanization for the dogs that were assigned the following reference or ID numbers in 2013: 1, 3, 4, 6, 8, 13, 23, 24, 25, 44, 65, 92, 94A, 94B, 103...

2.   The Invoice or Bill or Statement from [shelter vet clinic] showing services performed for the XXXXX Shelter from July 1, 2012 through August 31, 2013.

3.   Animal Intake and disposition reports related to the XXX Shelter from January 1, 2012 through August 21, 2013. These reports include but are not limited to Monthly Reports and Annual Reports.

4.   The receipt books and receipts of any kind from the XXX Shelter pertinent to animals that have been in the control and custody of the Shelter and that left the facility either as an adoption, rescue, return to owner, or court case from January 1, 2015 through August 31, 2017. These receipts must include funds collected from adopters, owners claiming their pets, fees paid by rescues, court fees, and all other animal-related fees collected.

I request a waiver of all fees for this request including but not limited to printouts and copies of information in response to this FOIA request dated [date of this FOIA]. Disclosure of the requested information to me is in the public interest, because it is likely to contribute significantly to public understanding of the operations or activities of the government and is not primarily in my commercial interest.

Specific explanation for waiver of fees: As a prominent person in the animal rescue community in [XXX] County and the City of [XXX], people ask me questions about the [your shelter] and its operations. People also ask me about their missing dogs and wonder if they have been killed at the facility.

Should a waiver of fees not be allowed, the maximum amount of fees I can pay is $20. Should fees exceed that amount, please let me know as soon as possible and I will schedule a time to come and physically copy the records for myself using my equipment.

Please also provide a fee schedule of any and all costs for which I would be responsible.

Please submit all questions about this request to me in writing through my email address: [your email].

You may notify me when and where the requested FOIA information is available by this email: [your email].

Please provide the requested records by [insert date – usually two weeks out].

Submitted by:
[Your name
Your address
Your phone number
Your email]

Appendix 2
Candidate Animal Welfare Questionnaire

This is just a sample. Use these as you see fit and be sure to add questions specific to your needs.

*****

Animal welfare issues are important to the 68% of Americans who own companion pets, and many more who simply care about animals. The XXXX Animal Shelter is a government department, funded by tax dollars, and should be run with the same professionalism as other government departments such as police and fire protection.

The citizens you want to represent want to know how you, as an elected official, will use their tax dollars and your position to improve the welfare of animals in your jurisdiction.

To that end, Reform Any City is submitting a questionnaire to all candidates during this election cycle to determine their positions on animal-related issues. Please return this survey by [date] to:

Address_____
Or
Email: _____

Your answers will be published on our Facebook page and may be used in our media and public relations information along with other candidates' responses. If you choose to not complete the survey, we will note that you provided no information.

Feel free to elaborate on any answer to ensure clarity.

Candidate name:
Office sought:
District:
Email address:
Telephone number:
Campaign website:
Facebook page:
Twitter account:

1. Are you a pet owner? If yes, please tell us about your pet(s).
2. Have you ever been involved in any animal-protection or welfare issues? If so, which ones and why?
3. Have you ever personally been inside our animal shelter? If so, when, and what were your opinions about what you saw?
4. If elected, what minimum standards of housing and care for shelter animals will you demand?
5. If elected, what improvements to the shelter's facility will you promise to work to make in a timely manner?
6. Are you aware of the live-release rate of the shelter for the last year? If so, what is your reaction to that rate?
7. If elected, what will you promise do to increase the live-release rate at the shelter and to actively work toward it becoming a No-Kill shelter within a year?
8. If elected, do you promise to ensure that all shelter animals are housed and cared for in a humane manner?
9. If elected will you ensure that volunteers are allowed to help care for and find homes and rescues for the shelter animals?
10. If elected will you ensure that volunteers are allowed to take photographs and videos of the shelter and the animals in it?

11. If elected, do you promise to make the shelter adhere to 42 U.S.C. § 1983, or Section 1983, that allows citizens to complain about and file violations about government-run entities such as animal shelters?
12. If elected, do you promise to create a position (staff or volunteer) within the shelter that will work with citizens and rescues to aggressively network shelter animals and make euthanization a last resort?
13. If elected, do you promise to be open to citizen questions, complaints and suggestions about the shelter, and to honestly investigate irregularities?
14. If elected, do you promise to publish the shelter's monthly intake and outcome statistics including the live-release rate, and number of adoptions, returns to owner, and rescues on the shelter's website?
15. If elected, do you promise to make all shelter records open and available to the public at all times, including records on specific animals as needed?
16. The shelter is currently open to the public for adoptions on weekdays during hours when most adults are working (Open: Tues, Wed and Fri 12:00 to 5:30). It is open to the public only 5 ½ hours each Saturday and Sunday. The shelter fails to run a comprehensive adoption program, including frequent and ongoing off-site adoptions in highly visible, high traffic locations, extensive marketing of at-risk animals, public-friendly adoption hours and mobile adoptions. If elected or re-elected, would you support a review and restructuring of the shelter's adoption program to include different, family friendly hours of operation as opposed to more hours of operation?

17. People frequently surrender animals to shelters when they perceive they cannot feed, train or medically care for them. If elected, will you support programs that have been proven to keep pets in their homes and out of shelters, such as surrender counseling, a pet food bank, pet behavior assistance, and distribution of heartworm preventative?

18. For years, the shelter has consistently returned only XX% of animals to their rightful owners. Conversely, some No Kill communities are able to return upwards of 60% of animals to their owners who want them back. If elected, will you support an internal review, and if necessary, a restructuring of the shelter's Return to Owner program?

19. Some dog breeds are being banned in many of the rental housing markets in our area. This makes finding appropriate housing very difficult for owners of these dogs, despite high levels of owner responsibility and great dog temperaments and training. This slows adoptions of these breeds and forces many owners to surrender their pets to shelters or abandon them. If elected, what steps would you take to reverse this ban, and to find solutions to this problem, in working with the apartment associations and property managers?

20. Animal welfare organizations have found that traditional "catch and kill" models are ineffective at addressing overpopulation. If elected, will you support the Trap, Neuter, and Return of healthy outdoor living cats to humanely and effectively reduce the population of outdoor cats and to reduce nuisance complaints?

21. To help ensure healthy, humane care of companion animals, do you support restrictions on pet stores that sell pets and large scale

commercial breeders ("puppy mills") that supply animals to those stores?

22. Although dogs were bred to be companion animals, many still live their entire lives at the end of chain. Not only do chained or "tethered" dogs suffer from loneliness, boredom, and anxiety, they also can become dangerously aggressive. Would you support legislation that would restrict the constant tethering of a dog (excluding times for exercise, outdoor fun, or potty breaks)?

23. If elected, would you allocate funds for free or low cost spay-neuter services in underserved areas?

24. Do you agree that there is a correlation between animal cruelty and violent crime?

Thank you for your participation. We look forward to your answers, and hopefully working together for improvements in the XXXX Shelter.

Appendix 3
Adoption Contract

In order to adopt a pet from AAAR, you must:

- Be at least 18 years old
- If you rent, must have approval from landlord
- Have identification with present address
- Be able and willing to provide a loving home for the pet
- Be able and willing to spend the money necessary to provide training, medical treatment and proper care of pet

Our Adoption fee is $200, which covers:

- Spay/neuter of pet
- All vaccines appropriate for age
- De-worming
- Micro-chip
- Heartworm test for dogs over 6 months old
- Dental if needed at time of spay/neuter
- Flea and tick preventative
- Heartworm preventative
- Any other medical needs
- Cat/Kitten adoption fee is $100

By adopting this pet, I agree that I am taking all responsibility for the pet from the date of adoption. I will provide any medical care needed and will not hold AAAR accountable for any medical issues that may arise after adoption. I will provide a safe, loving INDOOR home for said pet. All other pets in the home must be current on vaccines. If adopting a cat or kitten, I agree to not have my pet declawed.

I agree to notify AAAR if I cannot keep the pet and will return pet to AAAR. I will NOT relinquish to any shelter or person other than staff of AAAR. AAAR is not responsible for any damages, injuries or monies applied to pet while in adopter's care.

We are a rescue organization, and all adoption fees are considered donations and are nonrefundable 30 days after adoption. If the pet is returned within 30 days, the adoption fee except for $25 will be reimbursed to adopter, or it can be applied to the adoption of another pet if approved by AAAR. If paid by check, please allow 2 weeks to clear and then reimbursement will be mailed to you.

I understand that AAAR cannot guarantee the health, temperament, or training of the pet and hereby release AAAR from all liability once the pet is in my possession. The rescue makes no representation or warranties, expressed or implied, about the pet's temperament and is hereby absolved from any liability for future damages or injuries caused by said pet.

All pets in adopter's home are current on vaccinations and the adopter releases AAAR from any claim, cause of action or liability for any illnesses the adopter's other pets may develop, even if said pet's illness may have been procured from the adopted pet.

I further agree that I will keep the adopted pet on all preventatives and up to date on vaccines. As an adopter, I will comply with any laws in the municipality where the animal resides.

I will not allow the adopted pet to roam freely, and in the event that the pet were to get lost, I will contact an AAAR representative as soon as possible for further guidance. Identification tags must be kept on the adopted pet at all times.

In the event that it is discovered that the pet that I am adopting is harmed through my negligence or my failure to abide by the terms and conditions set forth in this agreement, I understand that I will be subjected to vigorous prosecution under the appropriate penal code in Tennessee or any other state and will be assessed all court costs pertaining to the recovery of the pet and any subsequent veterinary expenses incurred. I also understand that any expenses incurred by AAAR to reclaim said pet will be the responsibility of the adopter.

Furthermore, I agree that if the rescue must take action to have the title and possession of the pet returned to it, the adopter shall pay to the rescue a sum of $500 as liquidation damages, as well as attorney fees and court cost.

We enjoy getting updates on our adopted pets. By adopting from AAAR, you agree that a AAAR representative may contact you by phone, email or follow up visits.

Thank you for adopting one of our pets. Please feel free to contact us anytime with any questions.

By signing, you agree to all of AAAR requirements.

Signature of Adopter: _____

Date: _____

Signature of AAAR Representative:

_____

Made in the USA
Las Vegas, NV
14 December 2022

62004157R00090